DANIEL

२

DANIEL

A Difficult Book with a Message for Today

COLIN CHAPMAN

CASCADE *Books* • Eugene, Oregon

DANIEL
A Difficult Book with a Message for Today

Copyright © 2025 Colin Chapman. All rights reserved. Except for brief quotations in critical publications or reviews, no part of this book may be reproduced in any manner without prior written permission from the publisher. Write: Permissions, Wipf and Stock Publishers, 199 W. 8th Ave., Suite 3, Eugene, OR 97401.

Cascade Books
An Imprint of Wipf and Stock Publishers
199 W. 8th Ave., Suite 3
Eugene, OR 97401

www.wipfandstock.com

PAPERBACK ISBN: 979-8-3852-1196-8
HARDCOVER ISBN: 979-8-3852-1197-5
EBOOK ISBN: 979-8-3852-1198-2

Cataloguing-in-Publication data:

Names: Chapman, Colin [author].

Title: Daniel : a difficult book with a message for today / by Colin Chapman.

Description: Eugene, OR: Cascade Books, 2025 | Includes bibliographical references and index.

Identifiers: ISBN 979-8-3852-1196-8 (paperback) | ISBN 979-8-3852-1197-5 (hardcover) | ISBN 979-8-3852-1198-2 (ebook)

Subjects: LCSH: Bible.—Daniel—Criticism, interpretation, etc. | Dispensationalism. | Bible—Hermeneutics.

Classification: BS1555.52 C43 2025 (paperback) | BS1555.52 (ebook)

VERSION NUMBER 04/14/25

Quotations from *Daniel*, Volume 30 by John Goldingay. Copyright © 1996, 2019 by John Goldingay. Used by permission of HarperCollins Christian Publishing. www.harpercollinschristian.com

Scripture quotations marked (NRSV) are from the New Revised Standard Version Bible, copyright © 1989 the Division of Christian Education of the National Council of the Churches of Christ in the United States of America. Used by permission. All rights reserved.

Contents

Preface | ix
Introduction | xi

PART I: HOW DO WE DEAL WITH THE QUESTIONS OF INTERPRETATION AND AUTHORSHIP? | 1

1. How closely can some of the details in the visions be related to Antiochus Epiphanes? | 3
2. What is "the end" that Daniel is looking forward to? | 10
3. Is the fourth kingdom Greece or Rome? | 12
4. How does Daniel take up themes from other Old Testament books? | 15
5. How should we understand the numbers? Do we need to understand them literally? | 23
6. Is Daniel 9:24 looking forward to the restoration of the Jerusalem temple or the first and second comings of Christ? | 27
7. Does the structure of the book provide any clues to its interpretation? | 34
8. How are themes from Daniel taken up in the Gospels and Acts? | 40
9. How are themes from Daniel taken up in the Epistles and Revelation? | 52
10. Was the whole book written by Daniel in the sixth century BC, or was it written or compiled in the second century? | 63

Contents

PART II: HOW CONVINCING IS THE DISPENSATIONALIST INTERPRETATION OF DANIEL? | 71

1. "Daniel's prophecy needs to be interpreted literally, and this must include a literal interpretation of the numbers" | 73
2. "Daniel's prophecies make a clear distinction between the people of Israel and the church" | 76
3. "The inauguration of the kingdom of God and the coming of one like a son of man in 7:13–14 relate not to the first coming of Christ, but his second coming" | 78
4. "The second coming of Christ inaugurates the millennium, a literal period of a thousand years during which he reigns over the whole earth" | 80
5. "Daniel's visions look forward to the first coming of Christ, but then jump forward to the events leading to his second coming; they say nothing about the age of the church in which we are now living" | 83
6. "The fourth beast must represent Rome, not Greece; and the opposition to the reign of God at the end of the world will be led by a revived Roman Empire" | 86
7. "The restored temple in Jerusalem to which Daniel is looking forward is not in the period after the return from exile in 538 BC but in the end times" | 88
8. "References to the 'abomination of desolation' are all predictions of a future event in the end times, not to what Antiochus did to the temple in 167–164 BC or what Titus did in 70 AD" | 90
9. "Daniel contains several prophecies about the coming of the Antichrist" | 92
10. "Daniel's prophecies have begun to be fulfilled before our eyes in the Middle East through the return of Jews to the land and the creation of the State of Israel" | 95

Contents

PART III: WHAT IS THE MESSAGE OF DANIEL FOR TODAY? | 101

1. Daniel is a model for believers who engage with their context and their culture without compromising their faith | 103
2. God is Sovereign Lord of history; but human beings are still responsible for their actions | 107
3. Prayer is a vital way of cooperating with God | 112
4. God's people need to learn how to live in different political contexts | 116
5. While God sometimes delivers his people in miraculous ways, at other times they have to face persecution and suffering | 122
6. God has his own ways into the hearts of authoritarian rulers | 127
7. Christians need to take the task of biblical interpretation seriously | 133
8. Daniel has little or nothing to say about events in the Middle East in the twentieth and twenty-first centuries | 141
9. The hope that is based on the resurrection of Christ is greater and stronger than the hope that was offered to Daniel | 146
10. Daniel is a call to discernment, faithfulness, perseverance, and watchfulness | 150

Postscript | 156
Bibliography | 157
Subject Index | 159
Author Index | 163
Scripture Index | 165

Preface

Why would anyone who isn't a biblical scholar dare to write about the book of Daniel? It was while I was living with my family through the civil war in Lebanon (beginning in 1975) that I came across Ronald Wallace's *The Lord is King: The Message of Daniel* (IVP, 1979). I was greatly reassured by what Wallace saw as the basic message of the book—that history is never out of control, because God is at work in the rise and fall of nations.

When it became obvious that it was the presence of so many Palestinian refugees in Lebanon that had sparked off the civil war, I realized that I had to try to understand the Israeli-Palestinian conflict. And it was in that context that I wrote W*hose Promised Land?* (Lion, 1983), in which I tried to explain the history of the conflict and to challenge the way the Bible is used by many Christians to interpret the significance of the creation of the State of Israel.

My latest writing on these issues in *Christian Zionism and the Restoration of Israel: How Should We Interpret the Scriptures?* (Cascade, 2001) included a detailed study of Ezekiel chapters 34–48 and Zechariah, exploring how these books are interpreted in the New Testament and offering an alternative to the way they are interpreted by Christian Zionists. An American friend then suggested that I apply the same approach to the book of Daniel— another book that is used to support a particular understanding of "the end times" and events in the Middle East.

Preface

What's been happening in the world since I started studying Daniel—serious conflicts between nations, the rise of authoritarian regimes, financial crises, the widening gap between rich and poor, COVID-19, climate change, and increasing persecution of Christians—has created a situation in which many people "faint from fear and foreboding of what is coming upon the world" (Luke 21:26). So while trying to work out whether Daniel has anything to say about events in the Middle East in the twentieth and twenty-first centuries, I have come to appreciate that this biblical book has a powerful message that, while not directly addressing the question of modern Israel, speaks into some of our present anxieties.

Introduction

Every Children's Bible has to include the story of Daniel in the lions' den and the three men in the fiery furnace. But the rest of the book isn't nearly so appealing. The visions (which make up more than half of the book) are hard to understand and even harder to relate to our situation today. Do they describe events that would happen during and after the writer's lifetime, or several centuries later—or even at the end of the world?

It's impossible to avoid the difficult questions about authorship and date. Was the whole book written by Daniel during his time as a government official in Babylon in the sixth century BC? Or was it written by someone in Palestine in the second century? If the book comes from the sixth century, it means that the writer in Babylon was predicting events in the near future *in general terms* and predicting *in much greater detail* events which would take place in Syria, Palestine, and Egypt four hundred years later. If it was written in the second century, the writer or writers could have used traditional accounts of Daniel's visions and added similar visions to convey their interpretation of the brutal suppression that the Jewish people were experiencing under Antiochus Epiphanes.

Does it matter whether it was written in the sixth or the second centuries? It's easy to be so absorbed with the critical questions of who wrote the book that we fail to explore its message. My own conviction has been that addressing the difficult questions can help us to understand its message. Seeing the connections between the writer's context and our own context today may help us to hear the

Introduction

same message of encouragement that the author or authors of this book wanted to convey to their original readers.

We may need, for example, to be reminded of one major message of the book—that God is the sovereign lord of history: "the Most High is sovereign over the kingdom of mortals" (4:17). While God does sometimes deliver his people in miraculous ways, in other situations there is no deliverance from acute suffering. If Daniel was working as a top civil servant in a foreign country, he might have something to say to Christians working in a very secular world today. There could be a message of encouragement for Christians living under governments with a deliberate policy of discriminating against Christians. If God had his own way into the minds of powerful kings like Nebuchadnezzar, Belshazzar, and Darius, could he relate in the same way to the many autocratic rulers in the world today?

Part I, *How do we deal with the questions of interpretation?*, addresses some of the difficult question about authorship and interpretation. Instead of attempting to set out the whole range of different answers that have been offered (as in the many commentaries), I decided to explain the interpretations that I have found most convincing. Having begun in this way, I was encouraged to find that John Calvin adopted the same approach: "I do not usually refer to conflicting opinions, because I take no pleasure in refuting them, and the simple method which I adopt pleases me best, namely, to expound what I think delivered by the Spirit of God. But I cannot escape the necessity of confuting various views of the same passage."[1]

Part II, *How convincing is the dispensationalist interpretation of Daniel?*, explains why Daniel is a specially important book in this theological system that has influenced the thinking of many Christians since it was developed by John Nelson Darby in the 1840s. He taught that history has to be divided into seven distinct "dispensations," and that we are now living in the sixth dispensation and approaching the seventh dispensation (the millennium), a literal period of a thousand years in which Christ will rule the

1. Calvin, *Daniel*, 2:195–96.

Introduction

world from Jerusalem. In these chapters we discuss basic dispensationalist assumptions about the book of Daniel and suggest a more convincing interpretation using the principles of interpretation explained in Part I. Readers who have little or no interest in dispensationalism may want to skip Part II, and go straight to Part III.

Part III, *What is the message of the book for today?*, builds on the interpretation of Daniel explained in Part I, and suggests ways in which the book might speak to readers today. Having tried to understand the message of the book in the context—or contexts—in which it was written, does the book have a message for us in the world as it is at the present time? Each short chapter ends with a series of questions to prompt personal reflection or group discussion.

The title of this book conveys a "health warning": Daniel is a *difficult* book! If some readers have little interest in the difficult questions about authorship and interpretation, or in questions about dispensationalist interpretation of the book, they should go straight to Part III. This book presents some unique challenges, and there are major differences in the interpretations offered by devout and scholarly commentators. If some readers disagree strongly with my interpretations, I trust that they will concentrate on Part III. Understanding what God might have to say to us through this book today doesn't depend on our opinion on who wrote it and when! Our main question should be the question that was once put to Jeremiah: "Is there any word from the LORD?" (Jer 37:17).

PART I

How Do We Deal with the Questions of Interpretation and Authorship?

Introduction

Who wrote the book, and when was it written? Was it all written by Daniel in Babylon in the sixth century BC? If so, how was he able to predict in considerable detail what would happen in Palestine several centuries later? Or was it written in Palestine in the second century BC by someone who was living through a time of terrible persecution? If context is always so important for interpretation, what was the context—or the contexts—in which this book was written, and how can they help us to understand the message that it was intended to convey?

Why are some parts of the book in Hebrew and some in Aramaic? How should we interpret the mysterious numbers? Is the book looking into the immediate future or a more distant future—or even the end of the world? How does the writer take up themes from earlier books of the Old Testament? And how do the writers of the New Testament interpret Daniel?

Part I: How Do We Deal with the Questions

These are all difficult questions, and many different answers have been given. But trying to answer them may help us to understand the message of the book for today.

The following ten chapters deal with the main questions about where and when the book was written and how it should be interpreted.

1

How closely can some of the details in the visions be related to Antiochus Epiphanes?

There is universal agreement—even among scholars who believe that the whole book of Daniel was written in the sixth century BC—that many of the details in the visions fit perfectly with what we know about the life of Antiochus Epiphanes, the Seleucid ruler who dominated Palestine in the first quarter of the second century BC.

Ernest Lucas, for example, concludes that "There is no doubt that in ch. 8 the referent is Antiochus Epiphanes. Moreover, all the visions in Dan. 8–12 span the period from Daniel's day to the Antiochene era. It seems likely that the Antiochene era is the terminus of the vision in Dan. 7."[1] Later he goes so far as to say that "all Daniel's visions focus on the time of Antiochus Epiphanes."[2] Even Joyce Baldwin, a commentator who argues for a sixth-century date, writes concerning chapter 11: "There is universal agreement that Antiochus Epiphanes (175–63) fulfilled the description given here."[3]

What therefore is so significant about Antiochus Epiphanes? We know from the books of 1 and 2 Maccabees in the Apocrypha

---

1. Lucas, *Daniel*, 188.
2. Lucas, *Daniel*, 308.
3. Baldwin, *Daniel*, 212.

and from other historical sources that between 167 and 164 BC he engaged in "a systematic attempt to suppress the Jewish religion."[4] When some of his coins described him as *theos ephiphanous*, "God Manifest," and when he erected an altar to Zeus in the Jerusalem temple, this would have been seen by Jews as the ultimate blasphemy. John Goldingay points out that his actions "precipitated the greatest crisis in the history of the Judahites between the fall of Jerusalem in 587 and the events of the first century AD."[5] Wallace says that this crisis "involved the Jewish people in a life-and-death struggle for their survival and success in the service of God."[6] If Protestants had agreed with Roman Catholics in accepting 1 and 2 Maccabees within the canon of Scripture and read these books alongside Old Testament books, they might have been much more aware of this highly significant period of Jewish history between the Old and New Testaments.

This is the account in 1 Maccabees of the measures taken by Antiochus to abolish the sacrificial system in the temple, to stamp out the religious practices of Judaism, and to establish his own pagan religion:

> Then the king wrote to his whole kingdom that all should be one people, and that all should give up their particular customs. All the Gentiles accepted the command of the king. Many even from Israel gladly adopted his religion; they sacrificed to idols and profaned the Sabbath. And the king sent letters by messengers to Jerusalem and the towns of Judah; he directed them to follow customs strange to the land, to forbid burnt offerings and sacrifices and drink offerings in the sanctuary, to profane Sabbaths and festivals, to defile the sanctuary and the priests, to build altars and sacred precincts and shrines for idols, to sacrifice swine and other unclean animals, and to leave their sons uncircumcised. They were to make themselves abominable by everything unclean and profane, so that they would forget the law and change all

4. Lucas, *Daniel*, 254.
5. Goldingay, *Daniel*, 390.
6. Wallace, *Lord Is King*, 139.

How closely can some of the details in the visions be related

> the ordinances. He added, "And whoever does not obey the command of the king shall die . . ."
> Now on the fifteenth day of Chislev . . . they erected a desolating sacrilege on the altar of burn offering. . . . The books of the law that they found they tore to pieces and burned with fire. Anyone found possessing the book of the covenant, or anyone who adhered to the law, was condemned to death by decree of the king. . . . On the twenty-fifth day of the month they offered sacrifice on the altar that was on top of the altar of burnt offering. According to the decree, they put to death the women who had their children circumcised, and their families and those who had their children circumcised. (1 Macc 1:41–50, 54–61)

In a later chapter we have an account of how, after Antiochus' death, Judas Maccabeus led the resistance to Antiochus and restored the temple:

> Then Judas detailed men to fight against those in the citadel until he had cleansed the sanctuary. He chose blameless priests devoted to the law, and they cleansed the sanctuary and removed the defiled stones to an unclean place. They deliberated what to do about the altar of burnt-offering, which had been profaned. And they thought it best to tear it down, so that it would not be a lasting shame to them that the Gentiles had defiled it. So they tore down the altar, and stored the stones in a convenient place on the temple hill until a prophet should come to tell what to do with them. Then they took unhewn stones, as the law directs, and built a new altar like the former one. They also rebuilt the sanctuary and the interior of the temple, and consecrated the courts. They made new holy vessels, and brought the lampstand, the altar of incense, and the table into the temple. Then they offered incense on the altar and lit the lamps on the lampstand, and these gave light in the temple. They placed the bread on the table and hung up the curtains. Thus they finished all the work they had undertaken.
> Early in the morning on the twenty-fifth day of the ninth month, which is the month of Chislev, in the one

hundred and forty-eighth year, they rose and offered sacrifice, as the law directs, on the new altar of burnt-offering that they had built. At the very season and on the very day that the Gentiles had profaned it, it was dedicated with songs and harps and lutes and cymbals. All the people fell on their faces and worshipped and blessed Heaven, who had prospered them. So they celebrated the dedication of the altar for eight days, and joyfully offered burnt-offerings; they offered a sacrifice of well-being and a thanksgiving-offering. They decorated the front of the temple with golden crowns and small shields; they restored the gates and the chambers for the priests, and fitted them with doors. There was very great joy among the people, and the disgrace brought by the Gentiles was removed.... At that time they fortified Mount Zion with high walls and strong towers all round, to keep the Gentiles from coming and trampling them down as they had done before. (1 Macc 4:41–61)

These are accounts, written in the late second century, around fifty years after the events in Palestine and completely independent of Daniel, that describe the way Antiochus went about his attempt to wipe out the practices of Judaism, and how the temple was later restored. These are the tumultuous events that are referred to in the second half of Daniel. If, as most commentators believe, the "other horn" in Daniel 7 and the "another horn, a little one" described in 8:9–26 refer to the same person, this person must be Antiochus. It is generally agreed, therefore, that there are at least forty-four verses in the whole book of Daniel that refer to Antiochus—without of course mentioning his name. These are some of the key verses:

> As I looked, this horn made war with the holy ones and was prevailing over them.... He shall speak words against the Most High, shall wear out the holy ones of the Most High, and shall attempt to change the sacred seasons and the law. (7:21–25)
>
> Another horn, a little one, ... it took the regular burnt offering away ... and overthrew the place of the sanctuary.

How closely can some of the details in the visions be related

> Because of wickedness, the host was given over to it together with the regular burnt offering; it cast truth to the ground, and kept prospering in what it did. Then I heard a holy one speaking, and another holy one said to the one that spoke, "For how long is this vision concerning the regular burnt offering, the transgression that makes desolate, and the giving over of the sanctuary and host to be trampled?" (8:9–14)

> He shall make sacrifice and offering cease, and in their place shall be an abomination that makes desolate. (9:27)

> Forces . . . shall occupy and profane the temple and fortress. They shall abolish the regular burnt offering and set up the abomination that makes desolate. (11:29–31)

These and other verses refer to particular events during the lifetime of Antiochus that are described in greater detail in 1 and 2 Maccabees and other historical sources like Polybius, Appian, Livy, Josephus, and Porphyry:

- Antiochus gains power through intrigue (8:23; 11:21; 1 Macc 1:10).
- Antiochus is supported in Jerusalem by reformist Jewish leaders who cooperate with him (9:27; 10:27; 11:23, 32, 39; 1 Macc 1:11–15).
- The high priest Onias III is murdered in 171 (9:26; 2 Macc 4:30–34).
- Antiochus desecrates the temple by setting up an image of the god Zeus/Jupiter (8:11–12; 9:27; 11:30–31; 1 Macc 1:20–23, 54–59).
- Antiochus with his Seleucid army invades Egypt; but Rome intervenes and forces Antiochus to withdraw from Egypt (11:25–30; 1 Macc 1:16–19).
- Judas Maccabeus and his supporters resist Antiochus (11:34; 1 Macc 2–4)
- Antiochus is killed (8:25; 9:27; 11:45).

PART I: HOW DO WE DEAL WITH THE QUESTIONS

- After the forces of Antiochus are defeated by the Maccabees, the temple is re-consecrated in December 164 BC (8:14; 1 Macc 4:36–59), the event commemorated in the Feast of Hanukkah (meaning "Dedication").

One major objection which is raised about relating certain passages to Antiochus is that 11:40–45 looks as if it is a prediction of the fate of Antiochus, but happens to be completely inaccurate when compared with what we know from other sources about his death. This passage follows a detailed account of his activities (11:21–39), which fits well with what we know about him from other sources. How is it then that verses 21–39 seem to be an accurate account, whereas the following verses, 40–45, are totally inaccurate? We shall come back to this question in I.4 when we look at the ways in which Daniel's prophecies can be related to other books of the Old Testament. In the meantime, this is Goldingay's suggestion as to how to understand the difference between these two passages:

> Verse 40 marks the transition from quasi-prediction based on historical facts to actual prediction based on the Scriptures and on the pattern of earlier events. These verses, then, are not prediction in the sense of simply anticipatory announcements of fixed future events. Like the promises and warnings of the prophets, they paint an imaginary scenario of the kind of issue that God will ensure will come from present events. Their portrayal does not correspond to actual events of the 160s, as Jesus' coming does not correspond in a straightforward way to other OT prophecies of future redemption (e.g., Isa 9:2–7 [1–6]). It is not the nature of biblical prophecy to give a literal account of events before they take place.[7]

If, therefore, there is such general agreement that these passages fit with what we know about Antiochus Epiphanes, those who argue for a sixth-century date must attempt to explain why a writer in Babylon would write in such detail about events that would take place in Palestine four centuries later. Those who argue for a

7. Goldingay, *Daniel*, 545.

How closely can some of the details in the visions be related second-century date have to explain why the writer would use stories about Daniel in Babylon from earlier centuries to write about contemporary events in Palestine.

2

What is "the end" that Daniel is looking forward to?

"What's going to happen after him?" Goldingay suggests that this is the question in Nebuchadnezzar's mind when he has his first dream. "He's the great king who reigned over the Babylonian empire for forty years—for half its life. What's the future of this empire?"[1] When Daniel gives Nebuchadnezzar the interpretation of his dream, he tells him that "God has disclosed to King Nebuchadnezzar what will happen at *the end of days* . . . what is to be" (2:28–29). He goes on to speak of three kingdoms that will come after the Babylonian kingdom, and that will be followed by a very different kind of kingdom—a kingdom that will be set up by God himself and "that shall never be destroyed . . . and it shall last forever" (2:44). Jewish communities in Babylon would have been encouraged by the assurance that their painful experience of exile would not last for ever, because their God controlled the destiny of the Babylonian empire and all the empires that would come after it.

When Daniel has a similar dream sometime later during the reign of Belshazzar, the angel Gabriel tells him, "the vision is for the time of *the end*. . . . I will tell you what will take place later in the period of wrath; for it refers to the appointed time of *the*

---

1. Goldingay, *Daniel and the Twelve Prophets for Everyone*, 15.

What is "the end" that Daniel is looking forward to?

end" (8:17, 19). He then proceeds to speak about the kingdoms of Media, Persia, Greece, and the four kingdoms that will arise out of Greece (8:20–25). Daniel is told to "seal up the vision, for it refers to many days from now" (8:26).

In the second half of the book, "the end" seems to refer to something much more specific. Since, as we have seen in I.1, there is so much in these visions that can clearly be related to Antiochus, "the end" is probably the end of the suffering that the Jews were experiencing under Antiochus. In the visions relating to the conflict between "the king of the south" and "the king of the north," Daniel is told in a vision that "there remains *an end* (*qets*) at the time appointed" (11:28). The same word for "end" (*qets*) is used a further seven times (11:35, 40, 45; 12:4, 6, 9, 13). In 11:40 and 45 "*the end*" clearly relates to the war between the two kings. In 12:4 Daniel is told to keep the word secret and the book sealed "until the time of *the end*." In response to the question "How long shall it be until *the end* of these wonders?" (12:5), Daniel is given a mysterious number ("two and a half [years]" 12:7). This is followed by the assertion that "when the shattering of the power of the holy people comes to *an end*, all these things would be accomplished" (12:7). Since "all these things" probably refers to all the details of the visions described in chapters 10 and 11, it's natural to conclude that the writer is assuring his readers that Antiochus will not be able to maintain his control over the Jewish people for ever.

"The end" in Daniel, therefore, does not seem to be referring to a time in the far distant future or at the end of the world, but to particular events in the nearer future—particularly the end of Antiochus' brutal suppression and the rededication of the temple.

3

Is the fourth kingdom Greece or Rome?

The question here arises because the four beasts in Nebuchadnezzar's dream (2:31–45) are not identified. The fourth kingdom is described in more detail than the first three: "And there shall be a fourth kingdom, strong as iron; just as iron crushes and smashes everything, it shall crush and shatter all these; . . . it shall be a divided kingdom" (2:39–43). In Daniel's vision described in chapter 7, which has strong similarities to Nebuchadnezzar's dream in chapter 2, Daniel sees four beasts and is later told, "As for these four great beasts, four kings shall arise out of the earth" (7:17). Daniel then presses for more information: "Then I desired to know the truth concerning the fourth beast, which was different from all the rest, exceedingly terrifying" (7:19–20). In response he is told: "As for the fourth beast, there shall be a fourth kingdom on earth that shall be different from all the other kingdoms; it shall devour the whole earth, and trample it down, and break it to pieces" (7:23).

Does this fourth beast represent Greece or Rome? This is a significant issue because it has a bearing on the question of whether some of the visions relate to events in the second century BC or point beyond that time to the coming of Christ. Many early Christian commentators followed the Jewish historian Josephus and Jewish exegetes who believed that the fourth kingdom represented

Is the fourth kingdom Greece or Rome?

Rome. The four kingdoms were therefore seen as: 1. Babylon; 2. Medo-Persia; 3. Greece (Macedonia); 4. Rome. Lucas explains that "Early Christian scholars adopted this interpretation because, in their view, Jesus inaugurated the kingdom of God in the days of the Roman Empire."[1]

He points out, however, that in 2 Esdras 12:11–12, "a Jewish author writing at about the same time as Josephus, indicates that at that time this was a new interpretation that was only then beginning to replace an earlier one."[2] This suggests that Josephus' identification of the fourth beast as Rome was an innovation, and that the generally accepted interpretation before his time was that the fourth beast was identified as Greece.

Most scholars today believe that there is nothing in the description of the fourth beast that clearly identifies it as Rome. They therefore believe that the four kingdoms are: 1. Babylon; 2. Media; 3. Persia; 4. Greece (i.e., Alexander's kingdom of Macedonia). If the fourth beast represents Greece, therefore, the visions relating to the fourth beast describe the following major developments:

- The break up of Alexander's empire after his death in 323, leading to its division into four separate provinces, with Syria-Palestine being ruled by the Seleucids and Egypt by the Ptolemies ("at the height of his power, the great horn was broken, and in its place there came up four prominent horns," 8:8)
- The rise of Antiochus in 175 ("another horn appeared, a little one coming up among them," 7:8).

The book of Daniel is certainly looking forward to the coming of the kingdom of God on earth. But a major focus of the whole book seems to be the deliverance of the Jewish people from the rule of Antiochus. If the fourth beast is Greece and the kingdom inaugurated by Alexander, it is easier to understand why the visions seem to culminate in the time of Antiochus and

---

1. Lucas, *Daniel*, 190.
2. Lucas, *Daniel*, 77, 190.

Part I: How Do We Deal with the Questions

the Seleucid dynasty, which arose in Syria after the break-up of Alexander's empire.

4

How does Daniel take up themes from other Old Testament books?

Whether Daniel was written in the sixth or the second century, the writer or writers must have been familiar with many different books of the Old Testament. Writing about Daniel's visions, Baldwin comments "that they are not without their connections to the rest of the Old Testament, and . . . it is these connections which provide the original material out of which the visions have grown."[1] Similarly Goldingay comments that "the book of Daniel may well be the most intertextually determined and complex one among the books of the Hebrew Bible."[2] Tracing these echoes or reflections of other writers can sometimes shed light on the interpretation of difficult verses.

Many commentators have pointed out the similarities between the stories of Daniel in Babylon and Joseph in Egypt. Wallace spells out some of these parallels:

> When we read the first chapters of Daniel we cannot help noticing the parallels that can be drawn between Daniel at the court of Nebuchadnezzar and Joseph as the court of Pharaoh. Both men were exiles, showed exemplary

---

1. Baldwin, *Daniel*, 152.
2. Goldingay, *Daniel*, 129.

allegiance to God and his law, underwent deep humiliation through being falsely accused, and were ultimately vindicated. Both obtained recognition for their gifts through their ability to interpret an important dream which had greatly troubled their king, and which no other magician had been able to unravel satisfactorily. Both became confidants of the king and were given second place only to him in the government of the realm. Both men were recognized as having extraordinary gifts from God, were classed as outstanding among those who were "wise", and were associated with the other wise men of the court.[3]

Daniel's vision of one like a son of man in 7:13–27 contains echoes of the creation story in Genesis 1, where God creates humankind "in his image, in the image of God" and gives them authority to "have dominion . . . over every living thing that creeps upon the earth" (Gen 1:26–27). Baldwin makes the connection between the creation of humankind and Daniel's "son of man" in this way: "the one who comes with the clouds is like a human being in the sense that he is what every human being should be if he is true to type, that is, one who is made in the image of God" (Gen 1:26, 27). Commenting on the fact that the son of man is given not only "dominion," but also "glory and kingship," she says: "This second allusion to Genesis 1 indicates an enlarged status for the human race, greater than that which it received at the first, in the person of the representative 'man.'"[4]

These ideas, which are based on the creation story, help to explain the fact that, while the four kingdoms in chapters 2 and 7 are represented as *beasts*, the fifth kingdom, which God is going to establish, is a different kind of kingdom because it is represented by *a human being*. Lucas explains that this idea is

> probably rooted in the Hebrew understanding of humans as created in "the image and likeness" of God to have dominion over the animals. . . . It is when humans *image* God that they have a right to rule as his vice-regents. It is

3. Wallace, *Lord Is King*, 27.
4. Baldwin, *Daniel*, 159.

when they try *to be* God that they both forfeit that right and mar the image that distinguishes them from the animals. As a result, they become "bestial" to some degree. That the kingdom is given to a human figure, rather than to an animal one, asserts that when God acts to deliver his people and establish his kingdom he is consummating the purpose behind the creation of the cosmos. The vision affirms that "the God of *creation* is none other than the God of *redemption*" (Heaton). Once again we have the implied message that the redemption of humanity means not the destruction of the cosmos but the completion of the originally intended cosmic order.[5]

Three of the four kingdoms in Daniel's dream in chapter 7 are represented by wild beasts—a lion, a bear, and a leopard. Images of this kind appear in Mesopotamian and Canaanite mythology. But it has been suggested that the choice of these particular beasts may have been determined by a verse in Hosea where God speaks about his determination to chasten his people Israel: "I will become like *a lion* to them, like *a leopard* I will lurk beside the way. I will fall upon them like *a bear*, . . . there I will devour them like *a lion*, as *a wild beast* would mangle them" (Hos 13:7–8).

Daniel's prayer in chapter 9 is prompted by his recollection of the words of Jeremiah: "I, Daniel, perceived in the books the number of years that, according to the prophet Jeremiah, must be fulfilled for the devastation of Jerusalem, namely, seventy years" (9:2). This period of seventy years is mentioned in Jeremiah 25:11–12 and repeated in 29:10: "For thus says the Lord: Only when Babylon's seventy years are completed will I visit you, and I will fulfill to you my promise and bring you back to this place."

Is there any special significance in the number seventy? It could simply mean "a life-time." But the writer of 2 Chronicles, when quoting Jeremiah's prophecy about the exile lasting seventy years, relates it to teaching in the Torah about the need for the land to enjoy its Sabbaths:

---

5. Lucas, *Daniel*, 187, 200.

> He [God] took into exile in Babylon those who had escaped from the sword, and they became servants to him and to his sons until the establishment of the kingdom of Persia, to fulfill the word of the LORD by the mouth of Jeremiah, until the land had made up for its Sabbaths. All the days that it lay desolate it kept Sabbath, to fulfill seventy years. (2 Chr 36:20–21)

The writer of these verses in Chronicles must have in mind regulations like these in Leviticus: "the land shall observe a Sabbath for the LORD; ... in the seventh year there shall be a Sabbath of complete rest for the land, a Sabbath for the LORD; you shall not sow your field or prune your vineyard" (25:2, 4). If, however, the people disobey the law, they will be punished "sevenfold" for their sins: "If you continue hostile to me, and will not obey me, I will continue to plague you sevenfold for your sins" (26:21; cf. 26:24, 28). The ultimate punishment will be exile from the land:

> And I will scatter you among the nations, and I will unsheathe the sword against you; your land shall be a desolation, and your cities a waste. Then the land shall enjoy its Sabbath years as long as it lies desolate, while you are in the land of your enemies; then the land shall rest, and enjoy its Sabbath years. As long as it lies desolate, it shall have the rest it did not have on your Sabbaths when you were living in it. (Lev 26:33–35)

An exile that lasts seventy years will be part of the sevenfold punishment, and will be long enough to allow the land to enjoy the Sabbaths that it has not enjoyed because of the people's disobedience.

Leviticus 26, however, also speaks of restoration to the land after genuine repentance:

> But if they confess their iniquity and the iniquity of their ancestors, ... then I will remember my covenant ... and I will remember the land. For the land shall be deserted by them, and enjoy its Sabbath years by lying desolate without them, while they shall make amends for their iniquity, because they dared to spurn my ordinances. (26:40–43)

How does Daniel take up themes

Deuteronomy contains the same kind of assurance:

> When all these things have happened to you, the blessings and the curses that I have set before you, if you call them to mind among all the nations where the LORD your God has driven you, and return to the LORD your God, . . . then the LORD your God will restore your fortunes and have compassion on you, gathering you again from all the peoples. . . . Even if you are exiled to the ends of the world, from there the LORD your God will gather you, and from there he will bring you back. (Deut 30:1–5)

Daniel must have had passages like these in Leviticus and Deuteronomy in mind as he confessed the sins of his people and pleaded for restoration to the land. And his prayer is very similar to the prayers of Ezra and Nehemiah (Ezra 9:6–15; Neh 1:5–11; 9:5–37; cf. Ps 79).

Verses dealing with the Year of Jubilee in Leviticus 25 may provide a further clue for understanding the mysterious "seventy weeks" of 9:24. The law about the jubilee is explained in this way:

> You shall count off seven weeks of years, seven times seven years, so that the period of seven weeks of years gives forty-nine years. . . . And you shall hallow the fiftieth year and you shall proclaim liberty throughout the land to all its inhabitants. It shall be a jubilee for you: you shall return, every one of you, to your property and every one of you to your family. That fiftieth year shall be a jubilee for you: you shall not sow, or reap the aftergrowth, or harvest the unpruned vines. (Lev 25:8–11)

If, as most commentators agree, the "seventy weeks" mentioned in 9:24 means "seventy weeks of years," which is a total of 490 years, these 490 years are made up of ten Jubilee cycles, each of which is forty-nine years. Ideas about liberty, which are associated with the Jubilee, may therefore help to explain the angel Gabriel's message about how, during this period of "seventy weeks," God is going to answer Daniel's prayer for restoration to the land and for the restoration of the temple in Jerusalem.

Part I: How Do We Deal with the Questions

The strange reference to "ships of Kittim [Cyprus]" in a passage speaking about opposition to Antiochus (11:30) is probably a deliberate echo of a prophecy in Numbers 24:24: "But ships shall come from Kittim . . . and he also shall perish forever." It seems that an earlier prophecy about a power that "shall perish forever" is used here to predict the certain death of Antiochus.

The verses 11:40-45 present several problems because, as we have seen in I.1., while they seem to be predicting the downfall of Antiochus, "they do not correspond in any way with the events following his second withdrawal from Egypt and the beginning of the persecution of the Jews."[6] What we learn about his death from other sources, like 1 and 2 Maccabees and the historian Polybius, is totally different from what is described in these verses in Daniel. Goldingay argues that this passage

> is shaped as a whole as well as in specific detail by the OT tradition of the attack of a gentile foe who is defeated and killed near the gates of Jerusalem (e.g., Pss 2; 46; 48; 76), a tradition already reworked in prophetic passages such as Isa 10; 14:24-25; 31; Ezek 38-39; Joel 2:20; Zech 14, as well as by the prophetic portrayals of judgment on Egypt (Isa 19; Jer 43:8-13; 46; Ezek 29-32) and on Libya and Sudan (e.g., Nah 3:9, also Ezek 30:5).[7]

Following the same argument, Lucas offers a possible explanation of these difficult verses:

> Modern commentators tend to see in these verses evidence that vv. 2-39 are a quasi-prophecy, written after the events described, and that vv. 40-45 are looking forward to the downfall of Antiochus. The fact that these verses make more use than the preceding verses of phrases from the earlier prophets (especially Isaiah's prophecies regarding Assyria), and that some phrases are picked from earlier in the chapter, could support this. Here the seer's mind is illumined by motifs and phrases from Scripture rather than by his knowledge of

---

6. Lucas, *Daniel*, 290.
7. Goldingay, *Daniel*, 518.

How does Daniel take up themes

history.... If he is attempting a detailed prediction of the end of Antiochus' career, then he did get it wrong. However, the use of biblical phrases and the pattern he has constructed in the course of the historical survey suggest that he is doing no more than expressing in general terms the belief that, like other rulers before him who have given way to arrogance, Antiochus will meet an end befitting his blasphemous arrogance and his acts against God and against those who are faithful to God.[8]

There are several themes in Isaiah that are echoed in Daniel. Goldingay describes the visions as "coded history," and points out that "much of the 'code' comes from earlier Scripture, such as the books of Isaiah and Ezekiel. The vision thus shows it can make sense of the sequence of historical events by looking at them in light of Scripture."[9]

- Isaiah 40 begins with the message that the people in exile have paid the penalty for their sin, and are about to be restored to their land: "Speak tenderly to Jerusalem, and cry to her that she has served her term, that her penalty is paid, that she has received from the LORD's hand double for all her sins" (Isa 40:2). Gabriel's response to Daniel's plea for restoration after the exile emphasizes the fact that God has his way of dealing with sin: "Seventy weeks are decreed for your people and your holy city: to finish the transgression, to put an end to sin, and to atone for iniquity" (9:24). Both for Isaiah and Daniel, therefore, the restoration of Israel to the land after the exile means that "her penalty is paid," and that God wants his covenant people to enjoy his favor as they live in the land. Baldwin explains that "theologically the important point was that restoration marked acceptance with the Lord, who, by restoring his people to their land, demonstrated that he had forgiven and reinstated them (Isa. 40:1ff)."[10]

8. Lucas, *Daniel*, 293.
9. Goldingay, *Daniel and the Twelve Prophets for Everyone*, 58.
10. Baldwin, *Daniel*, 183.

PART I: How Do We Deal with the Questions

- There are several echoes of passages from the Servant Songs in Isaiah: for example, "those who are wise" (Hebrew *hamaskilim*) in 12:3 reflects the word *yaskil* (translated "shall prosper") in Isaiah 52:13; and "those who lead many to righteousness" in 12:3 reflects "the righteous one . . . shall make many righteous" in Isaiah 53:11.[11] If "those who are wise" were the kind of faithful Jews who contributed to the writing of the book, they may have seen themselves as playing the same kind of role as Isaiah's Servant of the Lord.

- In Isaiah 10:5-27 the prophet declares that after God has used the nation of Assyria as an instrument of judgment on Israel, he will then judge Assyria for the crimes they have committed: "When the LORD has finished all his work on Mount Zion and on Jerusalem, he will punish the arrogant boasting of the king of Assyrian and his haughty pride. . . . Destruction is decreed, overflowing with righteousness" (Isa 10:12; 22-23). Gabriel's response to Daniel's prayer seems to be quoting from Isaiah 10:22 when he writes: "Desolations are decreed . . . until the decreed end is poured out upon the desolator" (9:26-27). If this is the case, the writer of Daniel is taking words in Isaiah about God's judgment on Assyria (Isa 10:5-6, 12, 15) and applying them to his judgment on Antiochus. In the words of Lucas, therefore, "Antiochus is the 'new Assyria,' bringing havoc to Judah."[12]

These examples of what has been called "intertextuality" demonstrate how some of the most difficult passages in Daniel make much more sense when interpreted in the light of other passages in the Old Testament. It seems therefore that the writers of Daniel didn't treat earlier Scriptures simply as a set of predictions about what was to happen in the future. They learned from these Scriptures about how God works in history in order to understand how these patterns were being repeated in the history through which they were living.

11. Goldingay, *Daniel*, 518.
12. Lucas, *Daniel*, 284.

5

How should we understand the numbers? Do we need to understand them literally?

The Babylonian exile was to last for seventy years. Persecution was to last "time, two times, and half a time" [i.e., three and a half] (7:25; 12:7). "two thousand three hundred evenings and mornings" will elapse before the sanctuary is restored (8:14). "Seventy weeks are decreed for your people and your holy city" (9:24). The desecration of the temple is to last 1,290 days (12:11); and those who are faithful will persevere for 1,335 days.

Attempts to understand these numbers literally run into severe difficulties. In several cases it's difficult to work out when a particular period of time begins.[1] A further problem is that attempts in the past to identify particular prophecies in Daniel with important historical events inevitably appear to us now to be very misguided. These are several examples of such claims:[2]

- The prophecy given to Daniel in the year 538 BC about the restoration of the sanctuary and the beginning of the fifth kingdom (8:14) would be fulfilled in the year 1794, because this was 2,300 years after the prophecy was given to Daniel (Charles Wesley).

1. Goldingay, *Daniel*, 484; Lucas, *Daniel*, 235–36.
2. Goldingay, *Daniel*, 123–27.

- This same prophecy (8:14) predicted the year 1867, which marked the end of the temporal power of the Roman Catholic papacy (Henry Grattan Guinness).

- This same prophecy (8:14) was fulfilled in the Arab-Israeli war of June 1967, because it came 2,300 years after Alexander. This war was also a fulfillment of the reference to 1,335 days (12:12), because 1967 was 1,335 years after the establishment of the Islamic Caliphate.

- A fifth empire described in 2:41–43 should be identified as Islam, because it arose after the end of the fourth empire, Rome (E. W. Bullinger).

Few commentators today, therefore, insist on a literal interpretation of the numbers, and most believe that they need to be understood symbolically. Baldwin, for example, sees no need even to argue against literal interpretation and simply states: "The numbers are symbolic and not arithmetical."[3] If the numbers are to be interpreted symbolically, these are the most convincing interpretations that have been suggested:

- The period of seventy years for the exile can hardly be an exact figure, since if the exile began in 587 BC and the return to the land took place in 538, the exile lasted less than seventy years. The simplest explanation is that seventy years represents "something like a lifetime."[4] The Psalmist says "The days of our life are seventy years" (Ps 90:10), and Isaiah speaks of seventy years as "the lifetime of one king" (Isa 23:15). But, as we have already seen (in I.4), the seventy years probably also need to be understood against the background of Leviticus 26, which speaks about the need for the land to enjoy its Sabbath, and 2 Chronicles 36:20–21, which explains that the people were taken into exile from their land to enable the land to enjoy the Sabbaths that it was unable to enjoy during the years of Israel's disobedience.

---

3. Baldwin, *Daniel*, 190.
4. Goldingay, *Daniel and the Twelve Prophets for Everyone*, 49.

How should we understand the numbers?

- "A time, two times, and half a time" [i.e., three and a half] (7:25; 12:7) is the period of persecution of "the holy ones of the Most High." Lucas suggests that "As half the perfect number, seven, it denotes a short period of evil."[5] It is therefore an assurance that the period of persecution and suffering will not last for ever, but be strictly limited.

- The desecration of the temple is said to last for "two thousand three hundred evenings and mornings (8:14). This amounts to 1,150 days, which is a little longer than the period of Antiochus' desecration of the temple between 167 and 164 BC. Once again, according to Lucas, this is "probably a symbolic number for a short, significant period. This word of divine revelation adds specific comfort to the more general comfort to be drawn from the lesson of history. God is concerned with the detail of what is happening and, in this case, has put evil on a short rein."[6] The number of 2,300 therefore provides assurance that before long the temple will be restored.

- We have seen (in I.4) that the "seventy weeks" (*shavu'im shiv'im*) of 9:24 is generally understood to mean "seventy weeks of years." The simple arithmetic is therefore: 70 x 7 = 490. As we have seen the idea behind this number probably needs to be related to a passage in Leviticus 25 dealing with the Year of Jubilee, which is supposed to come after a period of forty-nine years. These "seventy weeks" therefore are linked to the "seven weeks of years" (*sheva shavtot*) in Leviticus 25:8, the forty-nine years after which the Year of Jubilee has to begin (25:8–17). These ideas associated with the Year of Jubilee and the land enjoying its Sabbaths can therefore help us to understand the "seventy weeks" described by the angel Gabriel in response to Daniels's prayer of repentance.

- In the last verses of the book, the period "from the time that the regular burnt offering is taken away and the abomination of desolation is set up" is said to last "one thousand two

---

5. Lucas, *Daniel*, 194.
6. Lucas, *Daniel*, 224.

hundred ninety days." This must refer to the length of time that Antiochus' desecration of the temple will last. This is followed by another puzzling number—1,335—which is 345 more than the 1,290 days: "Happy are those who persevere and attain the one thousand three hundred thirty-five days" (12:11–12). Lucas points out that "No-one has been able to suggest a satisfactory explanation of the two time periods given in vv. 11–12." After outlining three explanations that have been offered, he concludes: "The numbers may have some symbolic significance that is now lost to us. Whatever the actual meaning of the numbers, the significance of them is an encouragement to perseverance because the suffering has a time limit and will end fairly soon."[7]

If all these numbers need to be interpreted symbolically, we have to conclude that the writer was never intending to give a precise timetable of when certain events would take place. In the words of Lucas, "What this amounts to is not chronology but chronography . . . , the writing of a symbolic scheme of history which is intended to interpret major events in it, not to provide a means of predicting when it will happen."[8]

---

7. Lucas, *Daniel*, 298.
8. Lucas, *Daniel*, 284.

6

Is Daniel 9:24 looking forward to the restoration of the Jerusalem temple or the first and second comings of Christ?

Daniel 9:24 is the most problematic verse in the whole book. In his 1927 commentary, Montgomery wrote that "The history of the exegesis of the 70 Weeks is the Dismal Swamp of O.T. criticism." He also spoke of "the trackless wilderness of assumptions and theories" used in attempts to obtain "an exact chronology fitting into the history of Salvation."[1] In his commentary on Daniel John Calvin wrote about this verse: "This passage has been variously treated, and so distracted, and almost torn to pieces by the various opinions of interpreters, that it might be considered nearly useless on account of its obscurity."[2]

Daniel 9:24 is one complete sentence and includes three clauses that speak of God dealing with human sin and three that describe positively what he is going to do for the people of Israel and for Jerusalem:

> Seventy weeks are decreed for your people and your holy city:
> to finish the transgression,
> to put an end to sin,

---

1. Lucas, *Daniel*, 245–46.
2. Calvin, *Commentary on Daniel*, 195.

> and to atone for iniquity,
> to bring in everlasting righteousness,
> to seal both vision and prophet,
> and to anoint a most holy place [or thing, or one].

Many commentators in the past and present have seen this as prophecy that is looking forward to the work of Christ. Baldwin sums up this view when she writes:

> If we may tentatively interpret the verse, it is speaking of the accomplishment of God's purposes for all history. If we look at this from our vantage point it was accomplished in the coming of Christ, but it still has to be consummated (Eph. 1:10; 1 Cor. 15:28). If the historical work of Christ and his second coming are telescoped, this is not unusual, even in the New Testament.[3]

Wallace similarly sees the verse as looking forward to the whole of Israel's history:

> The language of this verse seems . . . a cool and calculated attempt to describe the ultimate consummation of Israel's history in an event of cosmic significance involving a coming Messiah and the destiny of all nations—the same kind of happening as that which great prophets like Micah and Isaiah and Jeremiah had already spoken about in their own varied terms. . . . [T]his passage describes much more fittingly what happened through the life, death, and resurrection of Christ.[4]

The alternative way of interpreting the verse is to understand it in the context of what comes before it and after it, and therefore to see it as a message addressed not only to Daniel and the Jewish community in Babylon, but also to the Jewish people in Jerusalem in the 160s BC. Verses 1–19 in this chapter record how Daniel turns to God in repentance on behalf of his people because he understands that the seventy years of exile predicted by Jeremiah have almost run their course. His prayer focuses on the future of

---

3. Baldwin, *Daniel*, 188–89.
4. Wallace, *Lord Is King*, 165.

looking forward to the restoration

Jerusalem and the temple: "let your anger and wrath, we pray, turn away from your holy city Jerusalem, your holy mountain.... For your own sake, Lord, let your face shine upon your desolated sanctuary.... O Lord, hear; O Lord, forgive; O Lord, listen and act and do not delay! For your own sake, O my God, because your holy city and your people bear your name!" (9:16, 17, 19). His main concern at the time of his prayer revolves around the return from exile and the restoration of the temple in Jerusalem.

We might therefore have expected that Gabriel's response to Daniel's prayer would speak about the return from exile and the restoration of the temple—events that are described in Ezra-Nehemiah. But the angel's response is a prophecy that looks much further ahead—far beyond the return to the land, which took place in 538, and the subsequent rebuilding of the temple. This amounts to what Goldingay calls "a prolonging of the Exile."[5] This is because, as Carol Newsom points out, "After the Persians defeated the Babylonian empire, Jewish political sovereignty was not restored. They remained a people subject to a new imperial power."[6] Lucas explains why it is that Gabriel comes to give Daniel "wisdom and understanding" (9:22) after his prayer: "Within the implied sixth-century setting of ch. 9, the point was not that Daniel did not understand the *meaning* of Jeremiah's prophecy, but that it had a *reference* beyond its most obvious reference to the ending of the Babylonian exile. It is this future reference that Gabriel comes to reveal to Daniel."[7] The prophecy of a return, which was originally related only to the Babylonian exile, therefore, is now being applied in a new way to a different situation several centuries later. Robert Anderson gives this explanation of why Gabriel's response is looking much further ahead than the return after the Babylonian exile:

> For the apocalyptist ... the difficulty lay not in the accuracy or near inaccuracy of Jeremiah's words, but in the fact that the expected state of bliss that was to follow

---

5. Goldingay, *Daniel*, Word Biblical Themes, 93.
6. Newsom, *Daniel*, 130.
7. Lucas, *Daniel*, 241.

on the return from exile did not eventuate. The nation that lost its independence in 587 B.C. did not regain it in 539. It merely changed one overlord for another, then another, and so on. While the yoke of Babylon had been removed, in keeping with the prophecy, a new and more uncomfortable one was waiting to be fixed.[8]

The angel tells Daniel that the "seventy years" of the exile are to be followed by "seventy weeks of years," in which the focus is on what is to happen to the temple. The last clause, "to anoint a most holy place" must refer to the consecration or re-consecration of the temple, and the first three clauses probably speak of the restoration of the whole sacrificial system, which dealt with "transgression," "sin," and "iniquity." In other words, says Goldingay, "It is the objective result in the sacrilege of the sanctuary that is Gabriel's concern." Daniel 9:24 is therefore "a restatement of the promises in ch. 8. Like that vision, it looks forward to the Antiochus crisis and promises God's restoration. . . . [V]v. 24–27 . . . do not suggest that the cleansing and renewal of which v. 24 speaks is the cleansing and renewal of the world: it is the cleansing and renewal of Jerusalem. The passage refers to the Antiochus crisis."[9]

Verses 25–27 in the same chapter spell out in greater detail how the prophecy in 9:24 will be accomplished during the period of seventy weeks of years:

- Weeks 1–7 (9:25a) cover the period from Jeremiah's prophecy (the 590s and 580s) up to the end of the exile. The "anointed prince" would then be either king Cyrus (who allowed the Jews in exile to return to the land), or the Zerubbabel (the governor in Jerusalem after the return), or Joshua the high priest (cf. Zech 4:14).

- Weeks 8–69 (9:25b), amounting to 62 weeks, include the rebuilding of Jerusalem (carried out under Ezra and Nehemiah) and the "troubled times" between then and the coming of Antiochus.

8. Anderson, *Daniel*, 111–12.
9. Goldingay, *Daniel*, 486–87, 497.

looking forward to the restoration

- Week 70 (9:26–27) includes five particular events in the time of crisis under Antiochus:

    a. The murder of the high priest Onias III in 171 BC ("an anointed one shall be cut off");

    b. Antiochus taking control of Jerusalem and the temple ("the troops of the prince . . . shall destroy the city and the sanctuary");

    c. Some Jewish leaders cooperating with Antiochus and his policies ("he shall make a strong covenant with many");

    d. The setting up of a pagan altar on which sacrifices were offered ("sacrifice and offering cease and in their place shall be an abomination that desolates"); and

    e. The death of Antiochus ("the decreed end is poured out upon the desolator").

Gabriel's response to Daniel's prayer, therefore, looks further ahead than the return from exile and includes the restoration of the temple after it has been desecrated by Antiochus. The "seventy weeks," the "seventy weeks of years," take us beyond the seventy years of exile, and cover the whole period from Jeremiah's prophecy about the return after the exile up to the end of Antiochus' rule and the re-dedication of the temple in 171.

But why are all these developments fitted into a scheme of 490 years? Having looked at echoes of earlier Old Testament books (in I.4) and understood how numbers are used (I.5), the simplest explanation of the 490 years ("seventy weeks") is that they make up ten Jubilee cycles, each of which is forty-nine years. This means that, just as the forty-ninth year leads up to the Year of Jubilee when slaves and captives were to be freed, so the 490 years will lead up to the glorious deliverance from Antiochus' oppression and the re-dedication of the temple. Lucas explains the difference between chronology and chronography as a way of interpreting this difficult verse:

Part I: How Do We Deal with the Questions

> A realization that Dan. 9:24–27 is chronography, and that it is based on jubilee cycles, indicates that what lies behind it is not a view of history as clockwork, but a recognition that there are patterns in history. In this case, the pattern is that of Yahweh's activity as the God who delivers his people from oppression. It was this truth about Yahweh that lay behind the Jubilee legislation (Lev. 25:38,55) and is central to Daniel's prayer.[10]

But if 9:24–27 refers *primarily* to events in the 160s, does this mean that we cannot see *a further fulfillment* many years after Antiochus? Jewish commentators in the first century AD saw a later fulfillment in the destruction of Jerusalem and the temple in 70 AD. And, as we have seen, many Christian commentators throughout the centuries have believed that the prophecy about God dealing with transgression, sin, and iniquity was fulfilled in the work of Christ on the cross. Are these legitimate ways of interpreting this prophecy in Daniel?

One way of answering this question is to suggest that there is no reason why these verses cannot be applied or re-applied to later situation *provided we recognize that they were addressed primarily to events in the 160s BC*. This view is well summed by C. E. B. Cranfield when he writes: "It seems . . . that neither an exclusively historical nor an exclusively eschatological interpretation is satisfactory, and that we must allow for a double reference, for a mingling of historical and eschatological."[11]

In this case we try to understand the events that these words were describing in their original context, and then recognize that the same pattern can be repeated in a later context. There is no reason why this same pattern cannot be repeated at a later time—and perhaps in a deeper and fuller way. So if God judged the arrogance and blasphemy of a ruler like Belshazzar, this must mean that he can judge any ruler at any time in history who demonstrates the same arrogance and blasphemy.

---

10. Lucas, *Daniel*, 253.
11. Quoted in Baldwin, *Daniel*, 223.

looking forward to the restoration

Throughout his commentary, Goldingay argues that those who put together the book of Daniel in its final form were addressing the Jewish communities in Palestine in the 160s BC. At the same time, however, he sees no reason why Christians should not see that these prophecies (like 9:24–27) can be related *also* to the coming of God's kingdom through the person of Christ:

> They do not suggest that the cleansing and renewal of which v. 24 speaks is the cleansing and renewal of the world: it is the cleansing and renewal of Jerusalem. The passage refers to the Antiochus crisis.
>
> Yet its allusiveness and the incompleteness of its fulfillment in the second century BC justifies its reapplication in later contexts. . . . Indeed, it directly encourages such reapplication by its not referring to concrete persons and events in the manner of a historical narrative such as 1 Maccabees. It speaks in terms of symbols of what those persons and events embodied, symbols such as wrongdoing, justice, an anointed leader, a flood, an abomination. It invites people to understand concrete events and persons in light of such symbols, but the symbols transcend them. They are not limited in their reference to these particular concrete realities. The symbols have other embodiments. . . .
>
> The fulfillment doesn't give people everything—the ultimate fulfillment will involve the ultimate implementing of God's final purpose. It does give them something, and something big, something that is the first installment of that final fulfillment. . . . God's act doesn't bring the actual end of everything, but it does bring an installment of the end, an embodiment within history of God's ultimate purpose and a confirmation that this ultimate purpose will find fulfillment.[12]

It's very understandable that Christians will look for everything they can find in the Old Testament that points forward to Christ. But if we're trying to make sense of the book of Daniel, it's vital that we first try to understand the message that 9:24 was intended to convey to those who first read it or heard it recited.

12. Goldingay, *Daniel*, 497; Goldingay, *Daniel and the Twelve Prophets for Everyone*, 41, 63.

7

Does the structure of the book provide any clues to its interpretation?

The most distinctive feature of the structure of Daniel is the way it separates stories from visions. Chapters 1–6 are stories about the fortunes of the Jewish people in exile in Babylon, focusing on the prominent role played by Daniel and his companions in public life and on two examples of miraculous deliverance. Chapters 7–12 include visions (relating to the future of the Babylonian Empire and the empires that will follow), which are recorded as visions seen by Daniel.

One unusual feature of the book is that chapters 1:1—2:4a and 8–12 are in Hebrew, while chapters 2:4b—7:28 are in Aramaic. Baldwin, following A. Lenglet, believes that the chapters in Aramaic "form a theology of history, addressed to the kings of the earth and therefore written in the international language [Aramaic] ... with the remaining chapters [8–12] written in Hebrew quite deliberately because they are addressed to the Jews."[1] She argues that chapter 7 marks the climax of the chapters written in Aramaic, and that it is "the high point in relation to the whole book." She quotes Lacoque who describes it as "the centre of gravity of the

---

1. Baldwin, *Daniel*, 67.

Does the structure of the book provide any clues

whole book," and "one of the summits of scripture."[2] This is the chapter in which judgment is passed on the four kingdoms, and the "son of man," representing "the saints of the Most High," comes into the presence of God to receive kingly authority and power.

Chapters 2–7 have a clear chiastic structure and "form a well-structured group":[3]

A A dream about four earthly kingdoms and God's kingdom (ch. 2)
  B A story about Jews being faithful in the face of death (ch. 3)
    C A story about royal hubris that is humbled (ch. 4)
    C^1 A story about royal hubris that is humbled (ch. 5)
  B^1 A story about a Jew being faithful in the face of death (ch. 6)
A^1 A vision about four earthly kingdoms and God's kingdom (ch. 7)[4]

In this structure the dream (A) and the vision (A^1) are both about four earthly kingdoms that will be followed by the establishment of God's kingdom. B and B^1 are both deliverance stories, while C and C^1 are judgement stories in which proud rulers are brought low.

This same chiastic structure is found in chapter 3:

A Nebuchadnezzar's decree to worship the golden image (vv. 1–7)
  B The Jews accused (vv. 8–12)
    C The Jews threatened (vv. 13–15)
      D The Jews confess their faith (vv. 16–18)
    C^1 The Jews punished (vv. 19–23)
  B^1 The Jews vindicated (vv. 24–27)
A^1 Nebuchadnezzar's decree honouring the Jews and their God (vv. 28–30)[5]

In this story, which begins with Nebuchadnezzar's decree ordering the worship of the golden image, the climax comes with the confession of faith on the part of the Jews. This then leads to

---

2. Baldwin, *Daniel*, 152–53.
3. Lucas, *Daniel*, 315.
4. Lucas, *Daniel*, 68.
5. Lucas, *Daniel*, 86.

a conclusion in which Nebuchadnezzar changes his mind and orders his people to honour the God of the Jews.

If chiastic structures can be traced in more than one section of the book, is it possible to find a chiastic structure in the book as a whole? Below is Goldingay's suggestion for how the book follows such a pattern:

1. Exile and the questions it raises: story
    2. A vision of four empires
        3. A trial of faithfulness and a marvelous deliverance
            4. An omen interpreted and a king challenged and chastised
            5. An omen interpreted and a king challenged and deposed
        6. A trial of faithfulness and a marvelous deliverance
    7. A vision of four empires
    (8. Aspects of this vision developed)
9. Exile and the questions it raises: vision
(10–12. Aspects of this vision developed).[6]

"Such chiastic structures," according to Goldingay, "feature in other ancient Near Eastern works."[7] Unfortunately they mean little or nothing to modern readers. Many English-speakers today do understand the structure and rhythm of a limerick. For example,

> There was a young man from Japan,
> Whose limericks never would scan.
> And when he asked why,
> He said "I do try!
> But when I get to the last line I try to fit in as many words as I can."

It's quite possible, therefore, that the those who first read the book of Daniel or heard it recited would have understood this chiastic feature of the structure of the book.

---

6. Goldingay, *Daniel*, Word Biblical Themes, 4.
7. Goldingay, *Daniel*, 575.

Does the structure of the book provide any clues

In the following chart the content of the five main dreams and visions in the book are set out side by side. In each column a summary of the dream is followed by the interpretation that is given. Setting out the dreams and visions in this way enables us to make the following observations:

- Chapters 2 and 7 cover the same period of time and end with God's intervention to bring the fourth kingdom to an end and establish his kingdom in the world.
- Chapters 7 and 8 offer some kind of interpretation of the four kingdoms in chapter 2.
- Chapter 2 has a broader picture of the great empires, while chapters 8–12 focus on the way the last of the four empires impacts the Jewish people.
- Chapters 8 and 11 begin at a later point than the earlier visions and cover only the Persian and Greek periods.
- In chapter 7, the persecution under Antiochus "appears as the main focus of the visions,"[8] and chapters 10–11 contain more detail about the persecution and about Antiochus' end.

---

8. Lucas, *Daniel*, 273.

PART I: How Do We Deal with the Questions

Nebuchadnez- zar's Dream	Daniels's Dream & Visions (1)	Daniels's Vision (2)	Daniel's Vision (3)	Daniel's Vision (3)
Chapter 2	Chapter 7	Chapter 8	Chapter 9	Chapters 10–12
603 BC (second year of Nebuchadnezzar)	552–21 BC (first year of Belshazzar)	550–549 BC (third year of Belshazzar)	539 BC	537 BC (third year of Cyrus)
A statue with head of gold, chest and arms of silver, middle and thighs of bronze, legs of iron, feet of iron and clay; a stone breaks the statue in pieces and becomes a mountain. Four kingdoms: head = Nebuchadnezzar of Babylon; kings 2 & 3 not named; 4th kingdom "strong as iron," but "a divided kingdom." "In the days of those kingdoms the God of heaven will set up a kingdom that shall never be destroyed. . . . It shall crush all these kingdoms and bring them to an end, and it shall stand for ever."	Four beasts come out of the sea: lion, bear, leopard; fourth beast "terrifying, dreadful and strong" and has ten horns. "Another horn appeared, a little one . . . speaking arrogantly." This horn makes war on the holy ones. A judgment scene in heaven before the "Ancient One"—dominion of the four beasts taken away: "one like a human being [a son of man] coming with the clouds of heaven. . . . To him was given dominion, glory & kingship." Four beasts are four kingdoms that will destroyed, and their kingdom given to "the holy ones."	A ram with two horns [Media and Persia]; a goat [Greece] grows great, but then broken; out of Greece come four horns (kingdoms) "Out of one of them came another horn, a little one"; "a king of bold countenance shall arise"; he "overthrew the place of the sanctuary . . . the transgression that makes desolate."	"Seventy weeks . . . for your people and your holy city." Weeks 1–7: lead up to the coming of "an anointed one." Weeks 8–69: the rebuilding of the temple.	"A great conflict" in heaven: Persia (with four kings) vs. Greece (led by "a warrior prince"). The kingdom of the prince of Greece divided between the "king of the south" (Ptolemies) and the "king of the north" (Seleucids). From the latter, "a contemptible person shall arise. . . . He shall . . . obtain the kingdom through intrigue." "They shall abolish the regular burnt offering and set up the abomination that makes desolate."

Does the structure of the book provide any clues

Nebuchadnez-zar's Dream	Daniels's Dream & Visions (1)	Daniels's Vision (2)	Daniel's Vision (3)	Daniel's Vision (3)
Chapter 2	Chapter 7	Chapter 8	Chapter 9	Chapters 10–12
		But "the sanctuary shall be restored"; "he shall be broken, and not by human hands."	Week 70: "an anointed one cut off;" destruction of Jerusalem; pagan altar and sacrifices; judgment on "the desolator."	"He shall come to his end." "At that time your people shall be delivered ... [and] the shattering of the power of the holy people comes to an end."
				"You [Daniel] shall rise for your reward at the end of days."

The structure of the book therefore emphasizes a conviction about the sovereignty of God in history and his purpose to establish his kingly rule in the world. It also underlines the significance of Antiochus and his oppression of the Jewish people at a vital stage in their history.

8

How are themes from Daniel taken up in the Gospels and Acts?

There can be little doubt that "the Son of man," which is the favorite title that Jesus uses for himself, comes from the book of Daniel. But this is not the only theme in Daniel that is taken up by the writers of the Gospels and Acts. Daniel therefore provides an important link between the Old and New Testaments, as Baldwin explains: "Daniel is seen to stand at the intersection between the Testaments, and at the crossroads of history. It is part of the considerable literature that bridges the gulf between the Old Testament and the New, and so provides a necessary preparation for an understanding of the ministry of Jesus."[1] Writing about Mark 13, Anderson comments that the chapter "contains some thirty instances of knowledge or use of the text of Daniel."[2]

There are at least six major themes in Daniel that are developed in different ways by the writers of the Gospels and Acts:

---

1. Baldwin, *Daniel*, 19.
2. Anderson, *Daniel*, 153.

How are themes from Daniel taken up in the Gospels

1. The coming of the kingdom of God

"The Lord is king," declares the Psalmist on many occasions (Pss 10:16; 29:10; 47:2, 7; 93:1; 95:3; 99:1; 97:1; 99:1). But it certainly doesn't look as if he is in control or as if humankind recognizes his sovereignty! So how, in the thinking of Old Testament writers, does Yahweh exercise his kingly rule? And is there any hope that his sovereignty will one day be recognized? The book of Daniel goes some way towards answering these questions and provides essential background for understanding how the writers of the Gospels understand the idea of the kingdom of God. "The theme central to Daniel as to no other book in the OT," says Goldingay, "is the kingdom of God."[3]

Daniel was a prominent official in the government of Babylon and would have been aware of what was happening in the kingdoms surrounding Babylon. This might explain why the word "kingdom" occurs fifty-four times in the whole book (forty-four times with the Aramaic *malku* or *malkuth* in chapters 2 to 7, and ten times with the Hebrew *malkuth* in chapters 8–12). Nebuchadnezzar's dream, as interpreted by Daniel, is about Babylon and the three kingdoms that will come after it, but goes on to describe a fifth kingdom of a very different kind: "In the days of those kings the God of heaven will set up a kingdom that shall never be destroyed, nor shall this kingdom be left to another people" (2:44).

After the incident of the fiery furnace, Nebuchadnezzar seems to recognize the sovereignty of God when he declares to all his people, "His kingdom is an everlasting kingdom" (4:3). In his second dream he is told that he will experience a breakdown "in order that all who live may know that the Most High is sovereign over the kingdom of mortals" (4:17). When he recovers from his breakdown he says: "I blessed the Most High. . . . For his sovereignty is an everlasting sovereignty, and his kingdom endures from generation to generation" (4:34). Belshazzar, on the other hand, is a king who refuses to recognize the sovereignty of God. The whole

---

3. Goldingay, *Daniel*, 581.

book of Daniel is therefore about the way God is at work in history and how he is going to establish his kingly rule in the world.

How then is the idea of the coming of the kingdom of God developed by the writers of the Gospels? The Gospel of Mark sums up the message of Jesus in terms of the coming of the kingdom of God: "The time is fulfilled, and the kingdom of God has come near" (Mark 1:15). The Greek word that is translated "has come near" (*engiken*) is the same word that is used in the same gospel to speak about the arrival of Judas in the Garden of Gethsemane: "my betrayer is *at hand (engiken)*" (Mark 14:42). Just as in the Gethsemane incident Judas was in sight, so now Mark is saying that in the coming of Jesus, the kingdom of God is in sight. After being challenged about the source of his power to heal, he declares, "But if it is by the finger of God that I cast out the demons, then the kingdom of God has come to you" (Luke 11:20). The book of Acts is book-ended by references to the kingdom of God, beginning with Jesus "speaking about the kingdom of God" in the period between his resurrection and ascension (Acts 1:3), and ending with Paul as a prisoner in Rome "proclaiming the kingdom of God and teaching about the Lord Jesus Christ" (Acts 28:31).

Nebuchadnezzar's first dream includes the picture of a stone that crushes the great statue: "a stone was cut out . . . and it struck the statue. . . . But the stone that struck the statue became a great mountain and filled the whole earth" (2:34–35). In Daniel's interpretation of the dream, the stone is the kingdom of God, which, unlike human kingdoms, can never be destroyed: "the God of heaven will set up a kingdom that shall never be destroyed, . . . just as you saw that a stone was cut from the mountain . . . and that it crushed the iron, the bronze, the clay, the silver, and the gold" (2:44–45). As Lucas explains, "it is clear that the stone symbolizes the establishment of the rule of the God of Israel centred in Jerusalem."[4]

This is probably the background to Jesus' enigmatic saying about the stone: "What then does this text mean: 'The stone that the builders rejected has become the cornerstone'? Everyone who falls on that stone will be broken to pieces, and it will crush anyone on

---

4. Lucas, *Daniel*, 79.

whom it falls" (Luke 20:17-18). This saying brings together three different passages from the OT: Psalm 118:22, Isaiah 8:14-15, and Daniel 2:44-45. As Goldingay comments, "Jesus speaks of himself as the stone that crushes, the very embodiment of the rule of God."[5]

If Daniel therefore is looking forward to the coming of the kingdom of God, the Gospels and Acts describe how Jesus claims that the time that Daniel and the prophets had looked forward to has finally come, and that through him the kingly rule of God is about to begin.

2. The kingdom of God and the Son of Man

The Aramic *kebar enosh* in Daniel's vision in chapter 7 is translated "one like a son of man" in the NIV, and "one like a human being" in the NRSV. But on the lips of Jesus the expression has become a title, and in most translations is therefore written with capitals: "the Son of Man." He claims, for example, that "the Son of Man has power on earth to forgive sins" (Mark 2:10), that "the Son of Man is lord even of the Sabbath" (Mark 2:28), and that "the Son of Man came to seek out and to save the lost" (Luke 19:10).

Jesus would have known the Psalmist's use of "son of man" to mean "a human being": "what is man, that you are mindful of him, and the son of man that you care for him?" (Psalm 8:4 ESV); "what are human beings that you are mindful of them, mortals [the son of man, *ben adam*] that you care for them?" (NRSV). He would have been aware that when the prophet Ezekiel is addressed ninety-three times as "son of man," it means nothing more than "human" or "man." On the lips of Jesus, however, the expression means much more than "a human being."

What therefore is so special about the expression in Daniel's vision, and what are the particular ideas associated with his "son of man" that are taken up and developed in the teaching of Jesus? In his first vision (ch. 7), Daniel sees a succession of four kings or kingdoms which are followed by "another horn," a figure that is

---

5. Goldingay, *Daniel*, Word Biblical Themes, 101.

generally understood to represent Antiochus. All these kingdoms, however, come to an end because "their dominion was taken away" (7:12). What happens in the court scene in heaven is that dominion passes from these kingdoms to "one like a human being [lit. 'son of man']," "one in human likeness":

> As I watched in the night visions, I saw one like a human being [a son of man] coming with the clouds of heaven. And he came to the Ancient of Days and was presented before him. To him was given dominion and glory and kingship, that all people, nations, and languages should serve him. His dominion is an everlasting dominion that shall not pass away, and his kingship is one that shall never be destroyed. (Dan 7:13–14)

The interpretation of the dream that follows suggests that the "son of man" isn't a single person, but that he has "both individual and corporate reference."[6] "As for these four great beasts, four kings shall arise out of the earth. But the holy ones of the Most High shall receive the kingdom and possess the kingdom forever—forever and ever" (7:17–18). "Whether collective or representative," writes Baldwin, "the term implies the creation of a community, a kingdom."[7] Before they "receive the kingdom," however, the saints have to endure intense suffering, since the following verses speaks of the Antiochus figure, who "made war with the holy ones and was prevailing over them. . . . He shall . . . wear out the holy ones of the Most High" (7:21, 25).

After this, final sentence is passed on "the horn":

> Then the court shall sit in judgment, and his dominion [i.e., the dominion of "the other horn," the figure representing Antiochus] shall be taken away, to be consumed and totally destroyed. The kingship and the dominion and the greatness of the kingdoms under the whole heaven shall be given to the people of the holy ones of the Most High; their kingdom shall be an everlasting kingdom, and all dominions shall serve and obey them. (7:26–27)

6. Goldingay, *Daniel*, 367–68.
7. Baldwin, *Daniel*, 168.

Giving "the kingship and the dominion" to the "son of man" involves giving dominion and kingship to "the people of the saints of the Most High." To explain the identity of the "son of man," Lucas writes, "it is clear that the kingdom envisaged is a restored Israel. ... It speaks of the ultimate downfall of the pagan powers and their replacement by God's kingdom, Israel."[8]

This must therefore be the picture that Jesus is referring to when he tells his disciples of his role as the son of man in the eschatological discourse: "Then they will see 'the Son of Man coming in clouds' with great power and glory" (Mark 13:26). At his trial before the Sanhedrin, when the high priest asked him, "Are you the Messiah, the Son of the Blessed One?" Jesus replies, "I am and 'you will see the Son of Man seated at the right hand of the power,' and 'coming with the clouds of heaven'" (Mark 14:62).

This saying about seeing the Son of Man coming in the clouds has traditionally been understood as describing the second coming. It is widely recognized now, however, that it needs to be related *primarily* to what was to happen in Jerusalem some forty years after Jesus' death. This is because what Daniel is describing is not a coming of the Son of Man *to earth*, but his coming *into the presence of God* to receive "dominion and glory and kingship, that all peoples, nations and languages should serve him" (Dan 7:14). Jesus refers to the Son of Man coming in clouds in the context of his prediction that Jerusalem is to be destroyed. He is therefore saying that the destruction of Jerusalem will be the culmination of a series of events following on from his death and resurrection—events that, taken together, will demonstrate that he has been vindicated and entered into the dominion and kingship that God has given him as the Son of Man.[9]

These ideas about the one like a son of man being a corporate figure must be the background to the surprising promise of Jesus when he offers the disciples a share in his kingdom: "You are those who have stood by me in my trials; and I confer on you, just as my Father has conferred on me, a kingdom, so that you may eat and

---

8. Lucas, *Daniel*, 77–78.
9. See Chapman, *Christian Zionism and the Restoration of Israel*, 168–70.

drink at my table in my kingdom, and you will sit on thrones judging the twelve tribes of Israel" (Luke 22:28; cf. Matt 19:28). C. H. Dodd points out the link between Daniel and this saying of Jesus: "The 'thrones' figure in Dan. 7:9, and the twelve as the nucleus of the new people of God, represent the 'saints' to whom judgment is given (Dan 7:22)."[10]

The closeness of the relationship between Christ and his disciples would explain why the risen Jesus challenges Saul on the road to Damascus with the words "Saul, Saul, why do you persecute me? . . . I am Jesus whom you are persecuting" (Acts 9:4–5). Because of the relationship between Jesus and his disciples, persecuting *them* means persecuting *Jesus himself.*

Could these ideas also be the source of the understanding of the relationship between Christ and the church that is expressed in his high-priestly prayer in John 17? He is praying that his disciples may become one with him and with the Father: "I ask not only on behalf of these, but also on behalf of those who will believe in me through their word. As you, Father, are in me and I am in you, may they also be in us. . . . The glory that you have given me I have given them, so that they may be one" (John 17:20–22).

It is through the Son of Man, therefore, that the kingly rule of God is established on earth, and the disciples of the Son of Man are in some way able to share in his kingdom. For these reasons Baldwin writes:

> Of all the figures used in the Old Testament to designate the coming deliverer—king, priest, branch, servant, seed—none is more profound than "Son of man." Here there is a vision of man as he was intended to be, perfectly embodying all his potential in obedience to his Creator. "Son of man" is also a term of glory, both in Daniel 7 and in Jesus's use of the term, but "the epiphany of the glory of the Son of man will be to those who have been proved by suffering" (J. Jeremias).[11]

---

10. Quoted in Baldwin, *Daniel*, 195.
11. Baldwin, *Daniel*, 171.

3. The suffering of the Son of Man

While Daniel's "son of man" is a figure of glory because he receives "dominion and glory and kingship" from God, he is also a figure who experiences suffering. This is because he represents "the people of the holy ones of the Most High" who suffer under ungodly rulers like Antiochus. Goldingay point out that "It is their suffering that brings about their attacker's downfall."[12] This must explain why Jesus' use of the title "Son of Man" is associated not only with glory, but also with suffering. Mark writes, for example, that after the transfiguration, "Then he began to teach them that the Son of Man must undergo great suffering" (Mark 8:31; cf. 9:12). The Greek word for "must" here (*dei*) is a strong word suggesting necessity and compulsion; this is something that *has to* happen.

Isaiah's figure of the Suffering Servant (Isa 52:13—53:12), therefore, isn't the only source in the Old Testament for Jesus' understanding that he would have to suffer. Such hints about the need for suffering are also found Zechariah's picture of the shepherd ruler who has to suffer: "'Awake, O sword, against my shepherd, against the man who is my associate,' says the LORD of hosts. 'Strike the shepherd, that the sheep may be scattered'" (Zech 13:7). These are the words that are quoted by Jesus when he tells his disciples that they are about to desert him: "Then Jesus said to them, 'You will all become deserters because of me this night; for it is written, "I will strike the shepherd, and the sheep of the flock will be scattered"'" (Matt 26:31).[13]

Another memorable saying of Jesus about the Son of Man emphasizes that he comes as a servant: "For the Son of Man came not to be served but to serve and to give his life as a ransom for many" (Mark 10:45). Daniel's "son of man" is given "dominion and glory and kingship, that all peoples, nations, and languages should serve him" (7:14). But Jesus knows that before he is exalted to the position where all peoples serve him, he has to take on the role of the servant and endure suffering and death.

---

12. Goldingay, *Daniel*, Word Biblical Themes, 91.
13. See Chapman, *Christian Zionism and the Restoration of Israel*, 156.

4. "The abomination of desolation"

Daniel refers to the altar dedicated to Zeus, which Antiochus erected in place of the altar in the Jerusalem temple, as "the transgression that makes desolate" (*hapesha shomem*, 8:13). Similar expressions are used on three other occasions ("an abomination that desolates" [9:27]; "the abomination that makes desolate" [11:31; 12:11]). The Hebrew *hapesha shomem* is generally understood as a parody of the Aramaic *Ba'al shamem* ("Lord of Heaven"), as Goldingay explains: "In the creative Jewish distortion of the name, 'rebellion' or 'abomination' replaces 'Baal,' . . . 'Desolating' replaces 'heavens,' using similar letters."[14]

While Mark and Matthew both quote Jesus' saying about "the abomination of desolation," it's only Matthew who refers to Daniel as the source of the expression: "So when you see the desolating sacrifice standing in the holy place, as was spoken of by the prophet Daniel (let the reader understand), then those in Judea must flee to the mountains" (Matt 24:15). The most natural interpretation of this saying is that Jesus is predicting the desecration of the temple that is still to come. He sees what is going to happen under the Romans as a repeat of what happened under Antiochus. The Romans would carry out in the temple the same kind of sacrilegious acts that Antiochus had carried out. Lucas explains that the Gospel writers don't see Daniel's references to "the transgression/abomination that makes desolate" as a *prediction* of what the Romans would do in the temple in Jerusalem in 70 AD, but rather *reapply* Daniel's words about what had happened in Jerusalem in the 160s BC to the actions of Titus:

> These reapplications do not imply that these later situations were what Daniels's visions were "really" about. Rather, it is because those visions involved insights into realities that transcend any one historical event, situation, or personage that they are open to reapplication. Such reapplication can be illuminating as the borrowed

---

14. Goldingay, *Daniel*, 424.

images acts as "lenses" and bring a particular perspective on the new situation to which they are applied.[15]

5. Divine judgment bringing tribulation

Jesus' warnings about the suffering that is to come echo Daniel's warnings about the suffering that his people will have to endure. There are similar warnings about the exceptional severity of the suffering, and similar words like "wrath" and "vengeance."

"There shall be a time of anguish, such as has never occurred since nations first came into existence." (Dan 12:1)	"For in those days there will be suffering such as has not been from the beginning of creation that God created until now, no, and never will be." (Mark 13:19)
"I will tell you what will take place later in the period of wrath."(Dan 8:19)	"For at that time there will be great suffering, such as has not been from the beginning of the world until now, no and never will be." (Matt 24:21)
"He shall prosper until the period of wrath is completed." (Dan 11:36)	
	"For these are days of vengeance, as a fulfillment of all that is written. ... For there will be great distress on the earth and wrath against this people." (Luke 21:22–23)

Goldingay reflects on the similarities between Daniel's visions and Jesus' eschatological discourse in Mark 13, Matthew 24, and Luke 21: "Jesus' discourse concerning the End speaks in Danielic fashion of troubling rumours, the final affliction, many stumbling, the need to endure to the end, the deliverance of the elect, the desolating sacrifice, the need to understand, and the coming of the human figure in clouds with great power and glory."[16]

---

15. Lucas, *Daniel*, 224.
16. Goldingay, *Daniel*, 107.

Part I: How Do We Deal with the Questions

6. Resurrection

While there are a number of places in the Old Testament where the writer expresses hope of life beyond death (e.g., Pss 16:9–11; 17:15; 49:15; 73:23–26; Isa 26:19), Daniel is unique in expressing belief in some kind of physical resurrection. This probably refers to a "general resurrection," since, as Baldwin suggests,

> The use of the word "many" in Hebrew is not quite parallel with its use in English. Hebrew *rabbim*, "many," tends to mean "all," as in Deuteronomy 7:1; Isaiah 2:2, where "all nations" becomes "many peoples" in the parallel verse 3: and in Isaiah 52:14, 15; 53:11, 12, where this keyword occurs no fewer than five times, with an inclusive significance.[17]

In the teaching of Jesus about the afterlife, as recorded by Matthew and John, there are clear echoes of Daniel:

"There shall be a time of anguish, such as has never occurred since nations first came into existence. But at that time your people shall be delivered, every one who is found written in the book. Many of those who sleep in the dust of the earth shall awake, some to everlasting life, and some to shame and everlasting contempt." (Dan 12:1–2)	"And these will go away into eternal punishment, but the righteous into eternal life." (Matt 25:46) "Very truly, I tell you, the hour is coming, and is now here, when the dead will hear the voice of the Son of God, and those who hear will live. For just as the Father has life in himself, so he has granted the Son also to have life in himself; and he has given him authority to execute judgment, because he is the Son of Man. Do not be astonished at this; for the hour is coming when all who are in their graves will hear his voice and will come out—those who have done good, to the resurrection of life, and those who have done evil, to the resurrection of condemnation." (John 5:25–29)

---

17. Baldwin, *Daniel*, 225.

How are themes from Daniel taken up in the Gospels

If the writers of the Gospels and Acts understood how the message of Daniel related primarily to situations in Babylon in the sixth century and in Palestine in the second century, they did not find in them clear *predictions* about the coming of Jesus. What they seem to have understood was that the life of Jesus reflected the same *patterns* as those that had unfolded in earlier centuries. They must have read Daniel as a book addressed primarily to the people to whom it was originally addressed. But they also believed that the book was looking forward to how God was going to act at a later time. It was in this sense that they could use the language of fulfillment. This approach is well summed up by Goldingay when he writes:

> One might express this point in another way by speaking of a typological relationship between the events and people of the Antiochene crisis and deliverance, and those of Jesus' time and of the End we still await. And it is in this sense that we can affirm the comment Pascal adds to an observation of the equivocal nature of the seventy weeks prophecy, that "we understand the prophecies only when we see the events happen."[18]

18. Goldingay, *Daniel*, 498.

9

How are themes from Daniel taken up in the Epistles and Revelation?

Epistles

Because Daniel's "son of man" is both an individual and a corporate figure, this could be the source of Paul's understanding of the church as the body of Christ. This idea is no doubt planted in his mind when the risen Jesus appears to him on the road to Damascus and challenges him with the words "Saul, Saul, why do you persecute me? . . . I am Jesus whom you are persecuting" (Acts 9:4–5). Because of the relationship between Jesus and his disciples, persecuting them means persecuting Jesus himself. Paul is therefore able to speak of "the church, which is his body" (Eph 1:22–23).

Daniel's last vision (chs. 10–12) begins with a description of "a great conflict," in which "events on earth reflect things happening behind the scenes in the heavens."[1] These ideas were no doubt in Paul's mind when he encouraged believers to "put on the whole armor of God. . . . For our struggle is not against enemies of blood and flesh, but against the rulers, against the authorities, against the cosmic powers of this present darkness, against the spiritual forces of evil in the heavenly places" (Eph 6:11–12). Paul was in

---

1. Goldingay, *Daniel and the Twelve Prophets for Everyone*, 53.

no doubt that, through his death and resurrection, Christ had won a decisive victory over all these supernatural forces, because "He disarmed the rulers and authorities and made a public example of them, triumphing over them" (Col 2:15).

Paul's portrait of the lawless man in 2 Thessalonians 2 seems to be modelled on the portrait of Antiochus in Daniel: "Let no one deceive you in any way; for that day will not come unless the rebellion comes first and the lawless one is revealed, the one destined for destruction. He opposes and exalts himself above every so-called god or object of worship, so that he takes his seat in the temple of God, declaring himself to be God" (2 Thess 2:3-4). This doesn't mean that Paul understood passages about Antiochus in Daniel as predictions of the Antichrist. Rather, as Goldingay comments, Antiochus in Daniel is "an actual, unpleasant reality in the life of the people of God. It is his reality that makes it possible for later generations to take him as a model for their portrayal of evil."[2]

Does the reference to "the temple of God" suggest that Paul was thinking about a literal temple in Jerusalem? F. F. Bruce explains why it is perhaps best understood as a metaphor:

> It may be best to conclude that the Jerusalem sanctuary is meant here by Paul and his companions, but meant in a metaphorical sense. Had they said, "so that he take his seat on the throne of God," few would have thought it necessary to think of a literal throne; it would simply have been regarded as a graphic way of saying that he plans to usurp the authority of God. This is what is meant by the language actually used here, although the sacral associations of *naos* imply that he demands not only obedience but also the worship due to God alone.[3]

Goldingay suggests that "The account of resurrection in 1 Corinthians 15 is . . . shaped by Daniel 7."[4] Both these passages, however, are shaped by the Genesis account of the creation of Adam. "The thought of Christ as the second Adam," says Leon Morris, "which

---

2. Goldingay, *Daniel*, 392.
3. Bruce, *1 & 2 Thessalonians*, 169.
4. Goldingay, *Daniel*, Word Biblical Themes, 102.

underlines this paragraph [in 1 Corinthians 15], is more fully developed in Romans 5. . . . Christ was truly a man as was Adam. It was fitting that, as it was *through a man* that corruption entered the race, so it should be *through a man* that it was overcome."[5]

Daniel was probably written to encourage believers facing persecution, and the book ends with an encouragement to perseverance: "Happy are those who persevere and attain the thousand three hundred thirty five days" (12:12). Similarly, 1 Peter was written to prepare Christians to face persecution: "Beloved, do not be surprised at the fiery ordeal that is taking place among you to test you, as though something strange were happening to you. . . . Therefore, let those suffering in accordance with God's will entrust themselves to a faithful Creator, while continuing to do good" (1 Pet 4:12, 19).

Revelation

There are several obvious similarities between Daniel and Revelation: they are both described as apocalyptic; they are both written for believers facing—or about to face—severe persecution and even martyrdom; they both have throne-room scenes in heaven in which a court passes judgment; and they both describe a conflict in heaven which is the background to conflicts on earth and in which God's victory is ultimately assured. If Daniel reached its final form in the second century BC, the oppressor confronting God's people was Antiochus. The writer of Revelation knew very well that the oppressor confronting the church at the end of the first century AD was Rome. Daniel was probably the latest book to be written and included in the Old Testament canon, while John was the latest to be written and included in the New Testament canon.

The major difference between the two books is that while Daniel is looking forward to the coming of the kingdom of God, John believes that the kingdom of God *has already come* through

---

5. Morris, *1 Corinthians*, 209–10.

the life, death, and resurrection of Jesus. Daniel is assured that when his people suffer and do *not* experience the miraculous deliverances recorded in the first part of the book, they can look forward to some kind of resurrection (Dan 12:1–2). But John knows what resurrection means because he has seen a vision of the risen Christ who has said to him: "Do not be afraid; I am the first and the last, and the living one. I was dead, and see, I am alive forever and ever; and I have the keys of Death and Hades" (Rev 1:17–18). He also knows that because of Jesus' victory over death, martyrs are already sharing in the victory that he has won (Rev 20:4–6).

John's indebtedness to Daniel is summed up by Goldingay when he writes: "No New Testament document is more thoroughly permeated with Old Testament phraseology and images than Revelation, and no Old Testament book influences Revelation more than Daniel."[6] This influence is seen in many of John's expressions, in the freedom with which John uses material from Daniel, and in the way he develops major themes in Daniel.

There are several examples of John using the same, or very similar, expressions or images as Daniel. G. B. Caird believes that "John expects his readers to know the Old Testament well enough to pick up his frequent allusions to it."[7]

Daniel	Revelation
"the God of heaven" (2:19)	"the God of heaven" (16:1)
"what will happen at the end of days" (2:28)	"what is bound to happen soon" (1:1)
"so that not a trace can be found" (2:35)	"leaving not a trace to be found" (20:11)
"thrown down some stars" (8:10)	"swept some stars" (12:3)
"the sanctuary . . . to be trampled" (8:13)	"trample over the holy city" (11:2)
"seal the vision" (8:26–27; 10:14)	"do not seal the vision" (22:10)
"for a time, two times, and half a time" (7:25)	"for a time, and times, and half a time" (12:14)
1,290 days (12:11)	1,260 days (11:2; 12:6); forty-two months (11:2; 11:3)

6. Goldingay, *Daniel*, Word Biblical Themes, 102.
7. Caird, *Revelation*, 11.

PART I: HOW DO WE DEAL WITH THE QUESTIONS

There is, however, no slavish copying of Daniel's visions. John doesn't treat any of Daniel's visions as predictions that have been fulfilled in the coming of Jesus, and there is no attempt to interpret the mysterious numbers in the visions. Commenting on the way John uses the Old Testament, Caird describes him as "an artist handling his material with creative originality, . . . with complete freedom from any literalness or pedantry. . . . The symbolism is drawn from the Old Testament, but modified to carry a radically new meaning."[8]

The clearest example of this freedom is the way in which John combines Daniel's vision of the son of man "coming with the clouds" (Dan 7:13–14) with Zechariah's prophecy about people seeing the wounded shepherd king (Zech 12:10—13:1): "Look! He is coming with the clouds; every eye shall see him, even those who pierced him; and on his account all the tribes of the earth will wail" (Rev 1:7). Daniel describes beasts arising from the sea (4:17, 25, 32), while John describes a monster arising from the abyss (Rev 13:10). The "ten horns" in Daniel's vision (7:24–27) represent the ten Seleucid kings who came before Antiochus. For John "the beast rising out of the sea, having ten horns and seven heads" (Rev 13:1), represents "either the puppet kings of client kingdoms [of Rome] or men potentially of imperial rank."[9] John's vision of the risen Jesus (Rev 1:4–5) is heavily influenced by Daniel's "Ancient of Days" and "son of man," and by the description of the angel who appears in Daniel 10 (vv. 5–6). John's monster, which symbolizes Rome, has the characteristics of all four of Daniels' beasts (17:12).

John was interpreting Daniel in the light of his understanding of what Jesus had achieved, because, as Caird suggests, "John believed that the prophecy of Daniel, along with other Old Testament prophecies, was about to have a new and richer fulfilment."[10] Baldwin makes the same point when she writes that what John

---

8. Caird, *Revelation*, 7, 234, 79.
9. Caird, *Revelation*, 163.
10. Caird, *Revelation*, 127.

How are themes from Daniel taken up in the Epistles

does is to "stage a final panorama of human history, by comparison with which Daniel is merely a kind of first draft."[11]

The coming of the kingdom

Nebuchadnezzar's dream, as interpreted by Daniel, looks forward to the time when "the God of heaven will set up a kingdom that shall never be destroyed" (2:44). In Daniel's first dream, this kingdom is associated with "the son of man," "one like a human being," who is given "dominion and glory and kingship, that all peoples, nations, and languages should serve him" (7:14).

John's understanding in Revelation is that in the coming of Christ, God really has begun to establish his kingly rule in the world. In one of his visions there are loud voices in heaven which proclaims "The kingdom of the world has become the kingdom of our Lord and of his Messiah, and he will reign forever and ever" (Rev 11:15). And "the twenty-four elders" worship God as they say, "We give thanks to you, Lord God Almighty, the One who is and who was, because you have taken your great power and have begun to reign" (Rev 11:16–17). Later a similar voice declares, "Now have come the salvation and the power and the kingdom of our God, and the authority of his Christ" (Rev 12:10). John believes that, while the final consummation of the kingdom of God has still to come, Daniel's vision of the coming of God's kingdom has begun to be realized.

The temple and its meaning

In response to Daniel's prayer for his exiled people and for restoration to their land, the angel Gabriel points forward to a time long after the return to the land. He assures him that "seventy weeks are decreed to . . . anoint a most holy place" (Dan 9:24) and promises that sacrifice and offering will cease "until the decreed end is poured out upon the desolator" (9:27). These assurances

---

11. Baldwin, *Daniel*, 64.

are generally understood to refer to the rededication of the temple after its desecration by Antiochus. Whether these words were written in the sixth or the second centuries, faithful Israelites would have been greatly encouraged by the confidence that they would once again have a functioning temple in Jerusalem.

The tabernacle and the temple were such vital institutions because they were symbols of God's desire to live among his people. God had instructed Moses to build the tabernacle with these words: "Have them make me a sanctuary, so that I may dwell among them" (Exod 25:8; cf. 29:45–46; Num 35:34). The same message was communicated to Solomon when he was building the temple in Jerusalem: "Now the word of the LORD came to Solomon, 'Concerning this house that you are building, . . . I will dwell among the children of Israel'" (1 Kgs 6:13; cf. 8:12).

When we come to John's vision of "a new heaven and a new earth" in Revelation, however, there is no need for a temple, because, through the incarnation, God has come to live among his people: "Then I saw a new heaven and a new earth. . . . I saw the Holy City, the new Jerusalem, coming down out of heaven from God. . . . And I heard a loud voice from the throne saying, 'Now the dwelling [Greek *skene*, 'tabernacle,' AV] of God is with men, and he will live with them.' . . . I did not see a temple in the city, because the Lord God Almighty and the Lamb are its temple" (Rev 21:1–3, 22). The incarnation of the eternal Word is "the real thing" to which the tabernacle and the temple were pointing. For this reason it's hard to understand the dispensationalist interpretation which requires the rebuilding of a real, physical temple in Jerusalem and the re-establishment of the sacrificial system before the second coming of Christ.

The cosmic conflict

One of the main characteristics of all apocalyptic is the idea of a supernatural conflict in which different forces in the heavenly world are struggling against each other. Daniel's final vision describes a supernatural conflict between Michael, "the great prince, the protector of your people" and "the prince of the kingdom of Persia" (Dan 10:12–21; 12:1). These visions reflect the idea that, in the words of Goldingay, "events on earth reflect things happening behind the scenes in the heavens."[12]

Revelation develops this theme in a distinctive way, since, in the words of Baldwin: "The book of Revelation takes up the theme of conflict from where the book of Daniel leaves it, and looks to a final confrontation with the powers of evil who war against the church."[13] This conflict between God and the forces of evil is described in Revelation as a conflict between Michael and "the dragon"—a conflict in which the dragon is decisively defeated:

> And war broke out in heaven; Michael and his angels fought against the dragon. The dragon and his angels fought back, but they were defeated, and there was no longer any place for them in heaven. The great dragon was thrown down, that ancient serpent, who is called the Devil and Satan, the deceiver of the whole world—he was thrown down to the earth, and his angels were thrown down with him. (Rev 12:7–9)

Victory through suffering

In Daniel's visions there are several references to the suffering endured by "the holy ones" at the hands of Antiochus: "this horn made war with the holy ones and was prevailing over them" (Dan 7:21); "he . . . shall wear out the holy ones of the Most High . . . and they shall be given into his power" (7:25); "they shall fall by the sword and flame, and suffer captivity and plunder" (11:33); "There shall be a time of anguish, such as has never occurred since nations first came into existence" (12:1); "when the shattering of the power of the holy people comes to an end" (12:7).

In Revelation, John is given a "revelation of Jesus Christ" (Rev 1:1) in order to prepare Christians in Asia Minor to face increasing

---

12. Goldingay, *Daniel and the Twelve Prophets for Everyone*, 53.
13. Baldwin, *Daniel*, 75.

suffering—and even martyrdom. In the passage about the cosmic conflict between God and "that ancient serpent, who is called the Devil and Satan, the deceiver of the whole world," we are told that it is through the suffering and death of Jesus and the suffering and martyrdom of his followers that God is able to defeat all the forces of evil: "They overcame him by the blood of the lamb and by the word of their testimony; they did not love their lives so much as to shrink from death" (12:12). Richard Bauckham explains that John's aim is

> to show that the decisive battle in God's eschatological holy war against all evil, including the power of Rome, has already been won—by the faithful witness and sacrificial death of Jesus. Christians are called to participate in his war and his victory—but by the same means as he employed: bearing witness to Jesus to the point of martyrdom. . . . The reason why, in the final period of world history, God will not deliver his faithful people by the slaughter of their enemies, as he did in the days of Moses, Elijah, and Esther, but instead will allow them to be slaughtered by their enemies, is that this is the way in which the nations will be brought to repentance and faith, and the sovereignty over them be transferred from the beast to the kingdom of God.[14]

The saints sharing in the victory of Christ

In Daniels's first vision he sees "one like a human being," "one like a son of man," coming into the presence of God to receive "dominion and glory and kingship" (Dan 7:14). When the dream is interpreted, we find that the son of man represents "the holy ones of the Most High," and that they therefore share in the kingship that is given to the son of man.

These ideas are developed in several of the messages of the risen Christ to the seven churches. The message to the church at Thyatira: "To everyone who conquers and continues to do my

14. Bauckham, *Climax of Prophecy*, 233–34.

works to the end, I will give authority over the nations; to rule them with an iron rod . . . even as I also received authority from my Father" (Rev 2:26–28). The church at Laodicea is assured: "To the one who conquers I will give a place with me on my throne, just as I myself conquered and sat down with my Father on his throne" (3:21). In John's vision of the millennium he sees those who have been martyred as sharing in Christ's kingly rule: "Then I saw thrones, and those seated on them were given authority to judge. I also saw the souls of those who had been beheaded for their testimony to Jesus and for the word of God. . . . They came to life and reigned with Christ for a thousand years" (20:4–5).

The high-priestly prayer of Jesus in John 17 is often interpreted as his prayer for unity among his followers in the church. But could it not also be a prayer that speaks about something new that is about to happen—the closest possible union between Christ and his disciples: "I ask . . . that they may all be one. As you, Father are in me and I am in you, may they also be in us" (John 17:20–21)?

Perseverance in facing suffering

If the book of Daniel was put together in its final form in the second century, its readers were facing the full force of Antiochus' persecution. The writer or writers were helping their people to discern the true nature of the conflict in which they were involved, and the book ends with an encouragement to persevere: "Happy are those who persevere" (Dan 12:12).

John was writing in prison because of his Christian witness, and was writing for fellow Christians who were facing persecution and martyrdom at the hands of the Roman state. The message of the risen Christ, therefore, to the church in Smyrna is: "Do not fear what you are about to suffer. . . . Be faithful until death, and I will give you the crown of life" (Rev 2:10). Similarly his promise to the church in Philadelphia is: "Because you have kept my word of patient endurance, I will keep you from the hour of trial that is coming on the whole world to test the inhabitants of the earth" (3:10).

These examples of John's use of expressions in Daniel, his freedom in adapting images, and his development of major themes provide ample evidence of the "creative originality" "with complete freedom from any literalness or pedantry" that Caird finds in Revelation. John draws his symbolism from the Old Testament—and especially from Daniel—but adapts it "to carry a radically new meaning."[15]

---

15. Caird, *Revelation*, 7, 234, 79.

10

Was the whole book written by Daniel in the sixth century BC, or was it written or compiled in the second century?

We have deliberately left this question to the end because our views about the authorship and date will depend to some extent on our answers to the previous nine questions relating to the interpretation of the book.

If the book comes from the sixth century, it means that the writer in Babylon was predicting events in the near future relating to the rise and fall of nations *in general terms* and predicting *in much greater detailed* events that would take place in Syria, Palestine, and Egypt four hundred years later. If it was written—or at least reached its final form—in the second century, the writer or writers could have used traditional accounts of the story of Daniel and his visions and added new, similar visions. Their purpose would have been to assure their people that God would soon bring to an end the brutal suppression they were experiencing under Antiochus Epiphanes. Since we know that he died in 164 BC, the book might have been written a few years before this actually happened—perhaps between 168 and 165 BC.

Which of these conclusions seems most convincing? Arguments about the authorship and date have often centred on questions about the language of the book and its historical accuracy. But another major issue has been about the nature of biblical prophecy, and in particular about the ways in which it predicts the future. Most of those who have supported a sixth-century date, for example, see no reason why God could not have revealed in great detail to Daniel in the sixth century what would happen later in the second century. They argue that the case for a second-century date is often based on the assumption that a person like Daniel could not, or would not, make detailed predictions about events that were to take place in a different place several centuries later. Baldwin, for example, writes that "an earthbound, rationalistic humanism has so invaded Christian thinking as to tinge with faint ridicule all claims to see in the Bible anything more than the vaguest references to future events."[1]

It is also argued that for a second-century writer to pass their work off as written by Daniel in the sixth-century must be nothing less than "fraudulent." Wallace says that "Many find it exceedingly difficult . . . to see it as other than fraudulent (however 'pious' their motive) to try to pass off one's book under another and more influential name."[2] And Baldwin speaks of "a fairly sophisticated fictional element in the book."[3]

Several recent commentators who argue for a second-century date, however, don't question the idea that God could predict events in the distant future in considerable detail, but ask whether this kind of predictive prophecy is consistent with what we know about how biblical prophecy works. Goldingay, for example, raises the question in this way:

> So was the book written in the sixth century or in the second (or somewhere in between)? Was it that God led sixth-century believers into writing stories that directly spoke to issues that concerned their situation in exile, and also gave them previews of events to unfold over the next four centuries which would be primarily relevant to Jerusalem in the second century? Or was it that God

1. Baldwin, *Daniel*, 205.
2. Wallace, *Lord Is King*, 19.
3. Baldwin, *Daniel*, 204.

led second-century believers to collect earlier stories of the faithfulness which Jews had experienced from God and showed to God, and gave them further revelations regarding their destiny now, which built on that earlier material and which they could add to it?

In discussing this question scholars have taken into account a number of factors such as the nature of the languages in which Daniel is written (a mixture of Hebrew and Aramaic with a number of words imported from Persian, Greek, and other languages). But the most significant determinant of their attitudes has been their attitude to that fundamental question of what God seems more likely to have done.

In my opinion the second view is much more likely.[4]

These are the kinds of arguments that are used to support this second view:

- The amount of detail that fits with the life of Antiochus, especially in chapters 10–12, makes the prophecy of Daniel quite different in kind from prophecy in other books of the Old Testament. These other prophets are frequently predicting the future—speaking about exile, for example, and the return from exile, and declaring God's judgment on foreign nations. But they never describe the future as precisely and in such detail as the career of Antiochus is described in Daniel. For this reason many scholars have used the words "quasi-prophecy" or "quasi-prediction" to describe the way Daniel writes about Antiochus. This means that the writers are giving their interpretation of *events that have already happened* by describing them as *events that are going to happen in the future*. Explaining this approach, J. Mayer writes that "Theologically, narrating history as if it were prophecy affirms that the events that unfold have been within the control and purview of God: 'all things past, present and to come are present unto God.'"[5]

4. Goldingay, *Daniel*, Word Biblical Themes, 9–10.
5. J. Mayer, *A Commentary upon All the Prophets* (1652); quoted by Goldingay, *Daniel*, 385.

Part I: How Do We Deal with the Questions

- There are other examples of writings from different parts of the ancient Near East that give an interpretation of recent and current events by presenting them as prophecy. "Quasi-prediction," says Goldingay, "has its background in Akkadian prophecies that are influenced by Mesopotamian divination."[6] Lucas explains further:

    > The Akkadian Prophecies seem to have been written *after* most of the events they describe. . . . [T]heir purpose was not to *predict* the course of history but to *interpret* it. . . . If the connection between the Akkadian Prophecies and the passages in Daniel is valid, it indicates that the importance of these passages is not in whether or not they predict events, but in the interpretation they give of history, and in particular, how past history bears on the situation dealt with at the end of the survey of history, and what might flow from it.[7]

- Quasi-prophecy is generally attributed to a well-known person of a previous generation and is generally therefore pseudonymous. If the practice of pseudonymity is questionable in modern contexts, it clearly wasn't seen in this way in the ancient world. While many writers describe pseudonymity as "forgery,"[8] Goldingay explains why it probably would not have been seen in this way in the ancient world:

    > There are no Old Testament parallels to the visions in Daniel, but ancient Near Eastern parallels to the visions in Daniel are pseudonymous quasi-predictions, not actual predictions of known authorship. Those parallels also suggest that there is no reason to assume that the authors were scoundrels perpetrating a scam and producing a forgery with the cynical intention of deceiving their hearers regarding the visions' origin. It is just as likely that the immediate hearers would have known how

6. Goldingay, *Daniel*, 574.
7. Lucas, *Daniel*, 272.
8. Walvoord, *Daniel*, 20.

to hear them.... We know that in the ancient world, and in the Hellenistic world in particular, pseudonymity was a common practice used for a variety of reasons—some unethical, some unobjectionable—for poetry, letters, testaments, philosophy, and prophecies. That pseudonymity is a rarer literary device in modern Western culture, especially in religious contexts, should not allow us to infer the God could not use it in another culture.[9]

- Prophecy in the Old Testament is never presented in a way that assumes that history has been pre-determined, and that human beings therefore have no freedom and no responsibility for their actions. Goldingay writes:

    When prophecy is predictive, what it says about the future is intended to give people at the time some hope for the future, not in order to predict precisely what will happen and when it will happen.... [T]he point about God's warning isn't merely to declare what's bound to happen. It's to challenge people to change so they escape God's judgment.[10]

    He also suggests:

    The significance of describing past history as pre-written is to declare that God is in control even of the inexplicabilities of history—the successes of the godless and the sufferings of the faithful—and even at moments when evil is asserting itself in a particularly oppressive way. Given the difficulty of viewing history as it unfolds as the direct will of God, the books declare that it was foreknown by God and in some sense willed by him. It is part of some pattern and purpose rather than being random and meaningless. Like other parts of Scripture, however, I assume that God's capacity to know about the events before they happen and to stay in control of the way they develop is not incompatible with the reality of human decision making and responsibility for them.[11]

9. Goldingay, *Daniel*, 569, 134.
10. Goldingay, *Daniel and the Twelve Prophets for Everyone*, 32.
11. Goldingay, *Daniel*, 558.

Part I: How Do We Deal with the Questions

- Giving Jewish exiles in Babylon in the sixth century a detailed preview of historical events that would take place four hundred years later in Palestine would not have been much help to them in the situation they faced at the time. How would it help them—or succeeding generations of Jews in Babylon—to be told about conflicts that would develop between Syria and Egypt centuries after their time or about marriage alliances that would be negotiated between these two kingdoms? Goldingay points out:

    > The God of the Bible characteristically speaks contextually, into situations rather than independently of them. Further, he reveals key truths about the End that are relevant to people's present lives but declines to give information of a concrete or dated kind, insisting that people live by faith. It is difficult to see how the God of the Bible would reveal detailed events of the second century to people living in the sixth, even though he could do so.[12]

- While prophecy frequently gives a general picture of the future, it is never specific and detailed enough to enable people to predict exactly how this history will unfold. No Jewish person, however wise and discerning, could have worked out from prophetic texts in the Old Testament that Jesus the Messiah would be born in Bethlehem, be crucified, and rise again in Jerusalem. It was only *after the event* that people could understand the real meaning and significance of the life of Jesus. It was only after the resurrection that Jesus "interpreted to them the things about himself in all the scriptures" (Luke 23:27). Irenaeus, in the second century AD, had this understanding when he wrote that "every prophecy, before its fulfilment, appears to people to be full of enigmas and ambiguities. But when the time has arrived and the prediction has come to pass, the prophecies have a clear and certain meaning."[13] Pascal wrote that "we understand the prophecies only when we see

12. Goldingay, *Daniel*, 570.
13. Goldingay, *Daniel*, 550.

Was the whole book written by Daniel

the events happen."[14] And Isaac Newton made the same point when he wrote that God gave the prophecies to Daniel "not to gratify men's curiosities by enabling them to foreknow things, but that after they were fulfilled they might be interpreted by the event," so that "the event of things predicted many ages before will then be a convincing argument that the world is governed by providence."[15]

- If the book was put together in its final form during Antiochus' oppression of the Jews, the writer could have been inspired by the stories of Daniel, as Goldingay suggests:

  > My guess is that he was familiar with the preceding stories about Daniel in chapters 1–6, and in particular with the vision of four regimes in chapter 2, and made them the first part of his book. Wondering how God was involved in the history that lay nearer his own day, he longed to encourage people whose faith was under pressure. God used that earlier vision in chapter 2 to inspire him with the revelations in the second part of the book. His sense of being inspired by Daniel's story and Daniels' earlier vision, and his sense that he was simply working out the implications of Daniel's vision, would explain why he attached his own visions (chapter 7–12) to Daniel's story and Daniel's vision (chapters 1–6).[16]

- Some have argued that the book must have been written between 167 and 165—that is, *before* the end of Antiochus' rule in 164 BC—because it was predicting his fall, although not describing in detail how it would happen.[17] Goldingay therefore suggests that this might also explain how the book came to be accepted as a genuine revelation from God and was therefore included in the canon of Scripture:

  > The fulfilment of the actual prediction in the latter part of these visions, of Antiochus' fall and Jerusalem's

---

14. Goldingay, *Daniel*, 498.
15. Goldingay, *Daniel*, 123.
16. Goldingay, *Daniel and the Twelve Prophets for Everyone*, 59.
17. E.g., N. W. Porteous, *Daniel* (1965); quoted in Baldwin, *Daniel*, 203–4.

deliverance and restoration, would be a key reason why the community recognized that they did come from God and that God has been watching over that pointless series of events.[18]

The revelations concerned the history of the time from Babylonian supremacy to the time of Antiochus and promised that God would put down the oppressor. God did so, which is likely the reason the community took the book of Daniel into its Scriptures—it had been proved to be a message from God.[19]

The strongest challenge to the way of interpreting Daniel explained in Part I comes from those who accept some form of dispensationalism. In Part II, therefore, we examine how the basic principles of dispensationalism are applied to Daniel and challenge them in the light of the approach developed in Part I. Readers who have little interest in dispensationalism should at this point go straight to Part III.

---

18. Goldingay, *Daniel and the Twelve Prophets for Everyone*, 59.
19. Goldingay, *Daniel and the Twelve Prophets for Everyone*, 4.

Part II

How Convincing Is the Dispensationalist Interpretation of Daniel?

Introduction

Readers who are not familiar with the term "dispensationalism" or have never come across this way of interpreting biblical history may want to skip these chapters and go straight to Part III.

Why do we need to discuss dispensationalist interpretations of Daniel? Well, Daniel is important for dispensationalists because they believe it provides a comprehensive preview of history until the second coming of Christ and the start of a literal millennium when Christ will rule over the earth. This, for example, is how John F. Walvoord sums up the importance of Daniel in his commentary on the book:

> Among the great prophetic books of Scripture, none provides a more comprehensive and chronological prophetic view of the broad movement of history than the book of Daniel. Of the three prophetic programs revealed in Scripture, outlining the course of the nations, Israel, and the church, Daniel alone reveals the details of God's plan for both the nations and Israel. Although other prophets like Jeremiah had much to say to the nations and Israel, Daniel brings together and interrelates

these great themes of prophecy as does no other portion of Scripture. For this reason, the book of Daniel is essential to the structure of prophecy and is the key to the entire Old Testament prophetic revelation.[1]

It's impossible of course to engage with all the different varieties of dispensationalist interpretations. There are many Christian Zionists—Christians who support Zionism and the creation of the State of Israel because of the way they interpret the Bible—who would not call themselves dispensationalists. The authors of the volume *The New Christian Zionism*,[2] for example, claim that their Christian Zionism is "not dispensationalism" and challenge the idea that "Christian Zionism is a fundamentalist fantasy associated with old-style dispensationalism." They also recognize the existence of a new "progressive dispensationalism." They do, however, still share some of the fundamental assumptions of the system.[3]

We also need to recognize that there are few scholars today who defend the whole dispensationalist system. This would explain why recent scholarly commentaries on Daniel hardly ever engage with typical dispensationalist interpretations. Ideas that are part of this system, however, are still widely accepted in popular versions of dispensationalism. In a recent book, *The Rise and Fall of Dispensationalism*, Daniel G. Hummel distinguishes between what he calls "scholastic dispensationalism," which he believes is now effectively dead, and "popular dispensationalism," which is alive and well and still very influential in many churches.

In what follows we interact with Walvoord's commentary on Daniel, published in 2012, which probably represents the views of many who hold to some form of traditional dispensationalism. We set out ten basic assumptions in his interpretation of Daniel and respond to each one in the light of the answers to the key questions of interpretation discussed in Part I.

---

1. Walvoord, *Daniel*, 10.
2. McDermott, *New Christian Zionism*.
3. McDermott, *New Christian Zionism*, 149.

1

"Daniel's prophecy needs to be interpreted literally, and this must include a literal interpretation of the numbers"

Assuming that the book was written in the sixth century, dispensationalists recognize that all of Daniel's prophecies about the three nations that succeeded Babylon were remarkably accurate, because they correspond so closely to what we know from other historical sources about events in the following four centuries. Where the prophecies *don't* correspond to known historical events, it is argued that they must be predictions that have yet to be fulfilled. Writing about 9:24–27, therefore, Walvoord says:

> In contrast to the rather clear fulfillment of verses 25–26, verse 27 is an enigma as far as history is concerned, and only futuristic interpretation allows any literal fulfillment. . . . If the expositor desires to follow the text meticulously . . . there is no alternative but to declare the entire seventieth seven as yet future, for there has been no seven-year period fulfilling the events of the prophecy, however labored the interpretation.[1]

---

1. Walvoord, *Daniel*, 284, 287.

Literal fulfillment allows for recognition of "the apocalyptic character of its revelation."[2] But it demands that numbers have to be interpreted literally. Thus, for example, the "seventy weeks" of 9:24 have to be interpreted as a literal period of 490 years. The first week of forty-nine years is said to cover the period of the rebuilding of Jerusalem; and the following sixty-two weeks is 434 years which cover the period up to the death of Christ. There is then a parenthesis after the sixty-ninth week which includes the present age of the church in which we now live. The seventieth week, according to Walvoord,

> begins with the introduction of a covenant relationship between the future "prince who is to come" [the Antichrist] and "the many," the people of Israel. This covenant is observed for the first half of the future seven-year period. Then the special liberties and protections granted Israel are taken away, and Israel suffers persecution in their time of great tribulation. The beginning of the last three and one-half years of Daniel's seventieth seven is marked by the desecration of the future temple, the cessation of the sacrifices, and the desolation of the Jewish religion. . . . The culmination of the entire prophecy of the seventy weeks is the second advent of Jesus Christ that closes the seventieth seven of Israel as well as the times of the Gentiles.[3]

One problem with literal interpretation of the numbers is that it's not always easy to determine when the different periods begin and end, and as a result, very different interpretations are put forward by different scholars. It also means that if a particular prophecy has clearly not been fulfilled in past history, it is assumed that it has still to be fulfilled, and will therefore be fulfilled in the end times. As we shall see in II.5, this approach means that in two crucial places in the prophecy (between 9:26 and 9:27, and between 11:35 and 11:36), we have to assume that the writer jumps forward to events that will take place in the distant future.

2. Walvoord, *Daniel*, 10.
3. Walvoord, *Daniel*, 290.

Daniel's prophecy needs to be interpreted literally

In our discussion about the interpretation of numbers in I.5 and about the relevance of other Old Testament passages in I.4, we have set out what these numbers could mean if they are seen to be symbolic rather than literal. In the key passage in 9:24–27, for example, if we interpret the numbers as symbolic and relate them to passages in Leviticus 25 and 26, what we have is a survey of the period between the return from exile and the end of Antiochus' oppression, together with an interpretation of the significance of these events.

2

"Daniel's prophecies make a clear distinction between the people of Israel and the church"

Dispensationalists generally insist that all the promises and prophecies in the Old Testament relating to Israel remain valid for all time. Even after the coming of Jesus, Israel has to retain its distinct identity for all time, and the church is not a continuation of Israel. This why Walvoord asserts that there are "the two major programs of God in the Old Testament, namely, the programme for the Gentiles and the program for Israel."[1] He also assumes that the situation in the New Testament is the same, and that the church is something new and distinct from Israel.

Daniel's prophecy therefore has little or nothing to say about the church. So, for example, in his discussion of Gabriel's answer to the prayer of Daniel in chapter 9, Walvoord emphasizes that the angel's response "specifically takes up prophecy as it applies to the chosen people. . . . This chapter is specifically God's program for the people of Israel. . . . The church as such has no relation to the city of Jerusalem, or to the promises given specifically to Israel relating to their restoration and repossession of the land."[2] This means that the "seventy years" described in 9:24–27 describe

---

1. Walvoord, *Daniel*, 187.
2. Walvoord, *Daniel*, 249, 270–71.

"God's 490-year future plan for the Jewish people and Jerusalem."[3] Similarly, chapters 10–12 "constitute Daniel's fourth vision, gathering together the significant threads of prophecy, especially as they relate to the Holy Land and to the people of Israel."[4]

It is hard to see how this understanding of the relationship between Israel and the church is consistent with the teaching of the New Testament. In several Old Testament books the writers look forward to gentiles being blessed and enjoying all the blessings of the covenant with Israel (e.g., Isa 19; 56:6–8; Ezek 47:21–23; Zech 2:11; 6:15; 8:22–23; 9:9–10; 14:16–19; Ps 87:1–7). Jesus looks forward to the time when "many will come from east and west and will eat with Abraham and Isaac and Jacob in the kingdom of heaven" (Matt 8:11–12). He also says "I have other sheep that do not belong to this fold. I must bring them also. So there will be one flock, one shepherd" (John 10:16). Paul writes that Jesus through his death has broken down "the dividing wall" that separates Jews from gentiles and "has made both groups into one . . . that he might create in himself one new humanity ['one new man,' NIV] in place of the two" (Eph 2:11–22). He assures gentile believers that "All of you are one in Christ Jesus. And if you belong to Christ, then you are Abraham's offspring, heirs according to the promise" (Gal 3:26–29). He speaks of gentiles being like "a wild olive shoot" that is grafted into Israel, "the rich root of the olive tree" (Rom 11:17–24). If gentile believers in Jesus are grafted into Israel, those of Israel who do not believe are like "branches that were broken off" (Rom 11:17–24). In Paul's thinking, therefore, the church is not completely separate from Israel, but is joined to Israel and therefore in continuity with Israel.[5]

---

3. Walvoord, *Daniel*, 296.

4. Walvoord, *Daniel*, 301.

5. See further Chapman, *Christian Zionism and the Restoration of Israel*, 77–88.

3

"The inauguration of the kingdom of God and the coming of one like a son of man in 7:13–14 relate not to the first coming of Christ, but his second coming"

According to Walvoord, the kingdom of God, which is the fifth kingdom in Nebuchadnezzar's dream and which replaces the four earlier kingdoms, "can only be fulfilled in any literal sense by a reign of Christ over the earth."[1] He describes Daniel 7 as "a broad summary of the times of the Gentile, with emphasis on the climactic events culminating in Christ's second coming to the earth,"[2] and "a vision of heaven at the time of final judgment of the nations."[3] The vision of a son of man "coming with the clouds of heaven" to receive "dominion, glory, and kingship" (7:13–14) describes the second coming Christ and the defeat of all God's enemies (7:15–27). Similarly "Daniel 9 presents Israel's history from the time of Ezra and Nehemiah to the inauguration of the kingdom from heaven at Christ's second coming."[4]

In our study of the way the writers of the Gospels, Acts, Epistles, and Revelation understood Daniel (I.8 and I.9), it was

1. Walvoord, *Daniel*, 89.
2. Walvoord, *Daniel*, 221.
3. Walvoord, *Daniel*, 202.
4. Walvoord, *Daniel*, 221.

The inauguration of the kingdom of God

argued that the Gospel writers clearly believed that the kingly rule of God had *already* begun to come in and through Jesus. Mark summarizes the message of Jesus with the words "The time is fulfilled, and the kingdom of God has come near" (Mark 1:15). Jesus responds to a challenge about how he has been able to work a miracle of healing by saying, "If it is by the finger of God that I cast out demons, then the kingdom of God has come near to you" (Luke 11:20). In the book of Revelation the hosts of heaven declare that "The kingdom of the world has become the kingdom of our Lord and of his Messiah, and he will reign forever and ever. . . . Now have come the salvation and the power and the kingdom of our God, and the authority of his Christ" (Rev 11:15; 12:10). The writers of the Gospels and Revelation, therefore, clearly believed that something very decisive had happened through the coming of Jesus and that the kingdom of God had begun to become a reality. The consummation of the kingdom is still to come; but they seem to have believed that Daniel's prophecies about the coming of this kingdom had begun to be fulfilled.

As we have seen earlier (in I.8), Jesus' words about people seeing "'the Son of Man coming in clouds' with great power and glory" (Mark 13:26) have traditionally been related to the second coming. But these words were spoken in the context of Jesus predicting the destruction of the temple, and therefore need to be related *primarily* to the whole sequence of events from his death and resurrection to the fall of Jerusalem in 70 AD. The main reason for this is that in Daniel's vision, the son of man is not coming *to earth*, but coming *into the presence of God* in order to receive "dominion and glory and kingship" (7:13–14). Jesus is not describing something that will happened at the end of the world, because he goes on to say, "Truly I tell you, this generation will not pass away until all these things have taken place" (Mark 15:30). When he speaks about the coming of the Son of Man, therefore, he is claiming that the whole sequence of events that are to unfold in the near future—ending with the destruction of the temple—will vindicate his claims and demonstrate that the kingly rule of God on earth has really begun.

4

"The second coming of Christ inaugurates the millennium, a literal period of a thousand years during which he reigns over the whole earth"

For Walvoord, when Daniel's "son of man" is presented before "the Ancient of Days" and is given "dominion and glory and kingship," this is a reference to "the millennial rule of Jesus Christ, . . . the eternal state where God is manifestly supreme in His government of the universe."[1] It is not until the millennium that Christ "is given a worldwide kingdom involving all peoples. . . . This kingdom is obviously the expression of divine sovereignty dealing dramatically with the human situation in a way that introduces the eternal state where God is manifestly supreme in His government of the universe."[2]

In his first vision described in 7:17–28, Daniel sees four kingdoms come to an end and replaced by a very different kind of kingdom—a kingdom in which the "son of man" is given "dominion, glory, and kingship, that all peoples, nations, and languages should serve him" (7:14). In discussing this chapter Walvoord applies a very literal interpretation to explain the nature of this fifth kingdom: "By its terminology verses 7:23–27 demand that,

---

1. Walvoord, *Daniel*, 206–7.
2. Walvoord, *Daniel*, 206.

The second coming of Christ inaugurates the millennium

for the fifth kingdom to overcome the fourth, the fifth must be a sovereign and political kingdom, whatever its spiritual characteristics. They demand that this be a future fulfillment, since nothing in history corresponds to this."[3] This literal fulfillment must be in the millennium.

While this is hardly the place for a full discussion about the millennium, the objections to this understanding of a literal millennium, which is based on a dispensationalist interpretation of Revelation 21, can be summarized in this way:[4]

- Revelation 20:1–6 is the *only* passage in Scripture that speaks about "the millennium." This passage must be interpreted in the context of the book, which is full of symbols needing to be interpreted. If all the other numbers in Revelation (like three, seven, and ten) seem to be symbolic, there is no reason why the number one thousand should be understood literally. It would be very questionable to base such an important belief on a single passage in a book that is full of apocalyptic symbols.

- There is no reference here to the return of Christ in his second coming, and nothing that relates the period of a thousand years to the second coming of Jesus.

- There is no suggestion that "the millennium" takes place *on earth*. John sees an angel "coming down from heaven"; but there is no suggestion that the angel is coming down *to earth* or that the binding of Satan and the martyrs sharing in the victory of Christ take place on earth.

- Those who hold to a literal millennium assume that every believer will be able to share in the millennium. But the main focus in this passage is on the *martyrs* ("those who had been beheaded because of their testimony to Jesus Christ"), and not on the whole church.

---

3. Walvoord, *Daniel*, 214–15.
4. Chapman, *Christian Zionism and the Restoration of Israel*, 91–92.

What if the fifth kingdom of Daniel's vision was not the millennium, but the kingdom of God, which began to come through Jesus? Since the four kingdoms in the vision are symbolized by beasts, and the fifth kingdom is symbolized by "one like a human being," this fifth kingdom must be of a completely different kind. Wasn't this the kind of kingdom that Jesus had in mind when he said: "many will come from east and west and will eat with Abraham and Isaac and Jacob in the kingdom of heaven" (Matt 8:11–12)? The fifth kingdom must be the kingdom of God which has already begun to be a reality and which includes people of all races who believe in Jesus.

5

"Daniel's visions look forward to the first coming of Christ, but then jump forward to the events leading to his second coming; they say nothing about the age of the church in which we are now living"

One of the basic assumptions of dispensationalism is that history is divided into seven "dispensations" or ages. The age in which we are now living is the sixth dispensation, the age of the church. This will end with the second coming of Christ, which will inaugurate the seventh and last dispensation, the millennium. Working within this framework, Walvoord believes that Daniel, writing in the sixth century BC, is presenting a survey of world history from the Babylonian empire to the first coming of Christ, but then moves immediately forward to the second coming and the millennium. The present church age is therefore seen as a hiatus or parenthesis:

> Daniel does not deal with the age between the two advents except for the time of the end.... Daniel's prophecy actually passes over the present age, the period between the first and second comings of Christ or, more specifically, the period between Pentecost and the rapture of the church.[1]

1. Walvoord, *Daniel*, 75, 85.

> The entire period from the death of Antiochus Epiphanes to the time of the end is skipped over with no reference to events of the present church age.[2]

In order to explain this hiatus and the absence of anything relating to the present church age, Walvoord argues that there are two places in Daniel's visions where we come to an end of the pre-predictions about Antiochus and the first coming of Christ and move forward to the end times:

- In 9:24–27 there is a gap between the end of the sixty-ninth week and the beginning of the seventieth week (i.e., between 9:26 and 9:27). The seventieth week is "separated from the earlier sequence of years and scheduled for fulfillment in the future in the seven years preceding Christ's second advent. . . . If the final seven years is still eschatologically future, it broadens the possibility of fulfillment to the second advent of Christ and events related to it such as the millennial temple."[3]

- Chapter 11:2–31 describes the rise of four Persian kings, Alexander the Great, and a line of Ptolemaic and Seleucid kings, ending with Antiochus Epiphanes. Verses 32 to 35 describe how his policies win over some in the Jewish community, but provoke the resistance that leads to the Maccabean wars. According to Walvoord, these verses "contain approximately 135 prophetic statements that have all now been fulfilled." However, "From verse 36 on, the prophecy leaps the intervening centuries to predict events related to the last generation prior to God's judgment of Gentile powers and rulers—prophecy that has yet to be fulfilled."[4] Verses 11:36–45 therefore contain a description of the rise and fall of the Antichrist. He is at first defeated by the "king of the north," but when he recovers, rules the world for a period.

---

2. Walvoord, *Daniel*, 329.
3. Walvoord, *Daniel*, 270, 274.
4. Walvoord, *Daniel*, 345.

Daniel's visions look forward to the first coming of Christ

There is absolutely *nothing* in the text of these two passages to suggest that between two sentences we move forward by many centuries into the future. The dispensationalist scheme has been worked out without reference to Daniel, and then imposed on the text of Daniel. The interpretation that has been outlined in I.5 offers a much more natural way of interpreting these texts. Thus 9:24–27 covers the time from Daniel right up to the restoration of the temple after the fall of Antiochus. And the whole of the passage from 11:21–39 can be related to what we know of the career of Antiochus.

We have also noted a possible explanation of the fact that 11:40–45 looks very different from the preceding verses and *doesn't* correspond to what we know from other historical sources about Antiochus' end: the earlier passage, 11:2–39 was written as an interpretation of events that had *already taken place*, while 11:40–45 uses figurative scriptural language, which had already been used in other books of the Old Testament to describe the fall of tyrants, in order to predict the fall of Antiochus *in the near future*.

6

"The fourth beast must represent Rome, not Greece; and the opposition to the reign of God at the end of the world will be led by a revived Roman Empire"

Walvoord writes that "The description of the fourth beast . . . more obviously corresponds to the Roman Empire than to the empire of Alexander the Great. . . . Conservative scholars with few exceptions generally identify the fourth beast as Rome."[1] We have already seen (in I.4) that this view was first held by Jewish writers, and adopted by Christians because they believed that it was during the time of the Romans that the kingdom of God, Daniel's fifth kingdom, began to come.

One reason supporting the identification of the fourth beast with Greece is that the marriage alliances referred to in 2:43 and 11:17 took place under the Seleucids, but not, as far as we know, under the Romans. Another reason is that if the fourth kingdom is Greece, all the visions in chapters 2, 7, 8, and 11 end with Greece and the kingdoms that arose after the death of Alexander. If the fourth kingdom is Rome, then two of the visions end with Greece and two with Rome. And if the fourth kingdom is Rome, it is difficult to identify the "ten horns" that belong to the fourth beast. Dispensationalists recognize that there were no ten kingdoms that

---

1. Walvoord, *Daniel*, 199, 196.

The fourth beast must represent Rome, not Greece

arose out of the Roman Empire. So because of their insistence on "literal fulfillment of prophecy,"[2] they have to relate this prophecy to future events and claim that there will be a revived Roman Empire in the period before the second coming of Christ, and that this empire will fight against Israel, the people of God, but finally be defeated by Christ: "ten actual kingdoms will exist simultaneously in the future tribulation period."[3]

> Daniel's prophetic vision takes human history up to the first coming of Christ when the Roman Empire was in sway, and then leaps to the end of the age when, in fulfillment of prophecy, the fourth empire [Rome] will be revived and suffer its fatal judgment at the hands of Christ as His second coming.[4]

These problems are avoided if the fourth beast is seen to represent Greece. Lucas explains that Greece could be seen as "different from all the others" (7:7, 19) because "Macedonia, under Alexander the Great, was the first non-oriental power to conquer the Middle East."[5] Jews in Palestine in the second century would have understood how Alexander's empire was "different from all the beasts that precede it" (7:7), and would have been aware that it was after his death that Syria and Palestine came under the control of the Seleucid dynasty.

---

2. Walvoord, *Daniel*, 285.
3. Walvoord, *Daniel*, 200.
4. Walvoord, *Daniel*, 209.
5. Lucas, *Daniel*, 190.

7

"The restored temple in Jerusalem to which Daniel is looking forward is not in the period after the return from exile in 538 BC but in the end times"

In Gabriel's response to Daniel's prayer in chapter 9, he says that a period of "seventy weeks" is decreed for Israel and Jerusalem in order to "anoint a most holy place" (9:24). This is generally understood to refer to a restored temple in Jerusalem. But for dispensationalists the prophecy of 9:24–27 is not looking forward to the restoration of the temple after the return from exile, but to a restored temple in the end times. Because Muslims took over the temple mount in the seventh century and built the Dome of the Rock and the al-Aqsa Mosque, dispensationalists believe that, since the prophecy in Daniel must be fulfilled literally, there has to be a rebuilt and functioning temple in Jerusalem before the second coming. Referring to Daniel's reference to "the abomination of desolation," Walvoord writes:

> The fulfillment of this prophecy [9:24] necessarily requires the reactivation of the Mosaic sacrificial system in a rebuilt temple in Judea. . . . The present occupation of Jerusalem by Israel may be a preparatory step to the reestablishment of the Mosaic system of sacrifices. Obviously

The restored temple in Jerusalem to which Daniel is looking forward

> sacrifices cannot be stopped and a temple cannot be desecrated unless both are in operation.[1]

But if, as we have seen in I.5, there are good reasons for seeing 9:24-27 as a prophecy not just about the restoration of the temple after the exile, but also about the restoration of the temple after its desecration by Antiochus, there is no need to believe that it has to be fulfilled literally before the second coming.

If New Testament writers believed that Jesus spoke of *himself* as the fulfillment of everything that the temple had represented (John 1:14; 2:13-22; Rev 21:1-27), it is inconceivable that they would have believed that the temple would one day have to be rebuilt. If the writer to the Hebrews believed that the death of Jesus had once and for all done away with the need for any further sacrifices (Heb 9:23—10:18), it is hard to understand why he could have believed that the temple would have to be rebuilt and the whole sacrificial system reestablished.

---

1. Walvoord, *Daniel*, 288-89.

8

"References to the 'abomination of desolation' are all predictions of a future event in the end times, not to what Antiochus did to the temple in 167–164 BC or what Titus did in 70 AD"

The three references to the "abomination of desolation" (9:27; 11:11; 12:11), according to Walvoord, have nothing to do with desecration of the temple either by Antiochus between 167 to 164 BC or by Titus in 70 AD. And when Jesus quotes this same expression (Matt 24:15), he is not predicting what the Romans will do when they capture Jerusalem in 70 AD and desecrate the temple. He is speaking about something that will happen in the future:

> According to Christ, there will be a clear-cut event referred to as the abomination of desolation, similar to the language of 9:27, which will occur in the period just preceding His second advent.[1]
>
> Christ's reference to the "abomination of desolation" (Matt 24:15) clearly pictures the desecration of the temple, here prophesied as a future event.[2]

---

1. Walvoord, *Daniel*, 288.
2. Walvoord, *Daniel*, 199.

References to the 'abomination of desolation' are all predictions

If, as we have seen in I.5, it makes good sense to see the "seventy weeks" of 9:24–27 as covering the whole of the period from Daniel in Babylon to the end of Antiochus' rule over Jerusalem, then the three reference to the "abomination that desolates" (9:27; 11:31; 12:11) seem a very appropriate way of describing the statue to Zeus that Antiochus erected on the temple altar. It seems very forced and unnatural to suggest that the "abomination that desolates" has nothing to do with Antiochus and only refers to an event in the end times.

9

"Daniel contains several prophecies about the coming of the Antichrist"

Walvoord recognizes that many verses of Daniel's prophecy fit with what we know of Antiochus from other historical records, and therefore sees these prophecies as being fulfilled in the life of Antiochus. But he also believes that there can be "dual fulfillment,"[1] when a prophecy or prediction can be fulfilled in one context and fulfilled a second time in a later context. At the same time he recognizes typology, where a pattern that works out in one context becomes a type or pattern that can be repeated in a different context. He also believes that because some of the descriptions of the Antiochus figure are so much more extreme than what we know of Antiochus, they must be seen as predictions of the Antichrist. Writing about 8:23–26, for example, he says:

> This difficult passage apparently goes beyond that which is historically fulfilled in Antiochus Epiphanes to foreshadow a future personage often identified as the world ruler of the end time—the Antichrist. In many respects this ruler carries on a persecution of Israel and desecration of the temple similar to what was accomplished historically by Antiochus. This interpretation of the vision may be regarded as an illustration of double fulfillment

1. Walvoord, *Daniel*, 239.

Daniel contains several prophecies

of prophecy or, using Antiochus as a type, the interpretation may go on to reveal additional facts that go beyond the type in describing the ultimate king who will oppose Israel in the last days.[2]

Similarly he suggests that, while the destructive activities of "the horn" in 7:19–27 may relate to Antiochus Epiphanes, the activities of the Antichrist will be "much more severe and extensive."

> He is described as a blasphemer and a persecutor of the saints. He will also attempt to "change the times and the law," that is to change times of religious observances and traditions such as characterize those who worship God. Critics relate this to Antiochus Epiphanes. While Antiochus may foreshadow the activities of the little horn of Daniel 7, the complete fulfillment will be much more severe and extensive.[3]

We have seen (in I.8) that Paul's description of "the man of lawlessness" in 2 Thessalonians 2:1–12 seems to be modelled on Daniel's description of Antiochus. We have also seen that a writer like Goldingay, who argues strongly for a second-century date, appreciates that it is perfectly legitimate for New Testament writers to see Antiochus as someone representing a type that can be repeated.[4] Nevertheless, there is a clear difference between the language of typology and the language of prediction. It is one thing to say that "Antiochus presents a type that can be repeated," but it is another thing to say that "prophecies about Antiochus go beyond the historical Antiochus and are in fact predictions of the Antichrist."

Paul sees "the mystery of lawlessness" embodied in an individual who will be destroyed at the coming of Christ. But 1 John speaks of "many antichrists":

> As you have heard that antichrist is coming, so now many antichrists have come. . . . Who is the liar but the one who denies that Jesus is the Christ? This is the antichrist, the one who denies the Father and the Son, . . .

2. Walvoord, *Daniel*, 244–45.
3. Walvoord, *Daniel*, 215.
4. Goldingay, *Daniel*, 436–38.

and every spirit that does not confess Jesus is not from God. And this is the spirit of antichrist, of which you have heard that it is coming; and now it is already in the world. (1 John 2:18, 22; 4:3–4).

In Revelation we read of "the Devil, or Satan" (Rev 20:2) and "the beast," who represents imperial Rome (19:19). But the word "Antichrist" doesn't appear, and there is no single figure who opposes God and his people. The book of Revelation therefore certainly doesn't understand Daniel as predicting the rise of a single Antichrist figure.

10

"Daniel's prophecies have begun to be fulfilled before our eyes in the Middle East through the return of Jews to the land and the creation of the State of Israel"

Walvoord insists that Daniel's prophecies (and especially 9:24–27) jump from the time of Christ to the end times, and that they have nothing to say about the church and the church age, but only about Israel. He also believes that these prophecies include clear predictions about what is likely to happen in the Middle East in the build-up to the second coming of Christ. His basic assumption here is that Old Testament promises and prophecies about Israel and the land have begun to be fulfilled in the return of Jews to the land in the Zionist movement and the establishment of the State of Israel. Having seen a restored Jewish state in the land, we can look forward to a rebuilt temple in which the whole sacrificial system will be re-established:

> Today, when attention is again being riveted upon the Middle East, and particularly upon Israel, these issues are not merely of academic interest because they are the key to the present movement of history in anticipation of what lies ahead.[1]

1. Walvoord, *Daniel*, 217.

Part II: How Convincing Is the Dispensationalist Interpretation

> For Christians living in the age of grace and searching for understanding of these difficult days that may be bringing to a close God's purpose in His church, the book of Daniel casts a broad light on contemporary events foreshadowing the consummation. If God is reviving His people Israel politically, allowing the church to drift into indifference and apostasy, and permitting the nations to move towards centralization of political power, it may not be long before the time of the end will overtake the world.[2]

> The present occupation of Jerusalem by Israel may be a preparatory step to the reestablishment of the Mosaic system of sacrifices. Obviously sacrifices cannot be stopped and a temple cannot be desecrated unless both are in operation.[3]

It isn't easy to see how Daniel's prophecy gives any hint about the creation of a Jewish state. For, as John Collins, observes, "Daniel says little even of the future Jewish Kingdom in earth and has no blueprint for a new administration."[4] What has happened therefore is that dispensationalism has created the one and only lens through which we are asked to see the history of the last one hundred and forty years in the Middle East. In this way of thinking, there is no need to study the origins of the Zionist movement and the stages by which Jewish settlers gradually increased in numbers and power until they created the State of Israel. There is no need to ask why the Palestinians began to resist this settler movement and why conflict was almost inevitable. If the Old Testament gives Jews a divine right to the land for all time, and if their return to the land and the creation of the State of Israel were part of God's plan for the end times, this overrides any rights that Palestinians believe they have on the basis of centuries of occupation and any desires they may have for self-determination.

---

2. Walvoord, *Daniel*, 382–83.
3. Walvoord, *Daniel*, 288–89.
4. Collins, *Daniel*, 66.

Daniel's prophecies have begun to be fulfilled

An alternative way of interpreting Scripture, which we have used in Part I and elsewhere,[5] starts with the assumption that instead of reading the New Testament through the eyes of the Old Testament, we read the Old Testament through the eyes of the New Testament. We begin by understanding promises in the Old Testament about the nation and the land and thus appreciating the hopes and expectations of Jews at the time of Christ. We then go on to ask how the writers of the New Testament began to understand and re-interpret these typical Jewish hopes in the light of the coming of Jesus. They seem to have believed that all the Old Testament promises and prophecies both about the nation and about the land had been fulfilled through the coming of the kingdom of God in Jesus. Gentiles who believe in Jesus are therefore incorporated into the nation of Israel and inherit all the promises and blessings that had been given to Abraham. The universal church, which includes both Jews and gentiles has now become "the Israel of God" (Gal 6:16).

When this understanding of Scripture is applied to recent history in the Middle East, we start by recognizing that the restoration of millions of Jews back to the land and the creation of the State of Israel have happened under the sovereignty of God. But this does not mean that these events should be seen as *the* fulfillment, or even as *a* fulfillment, of biblical promises and prophecies about the nation and the land. The book of Daniel and the Bible as a whole do *not* provide us with a step-by-step programme of how history will unfold in the Middle East before the second coming of Jesus.[6]

When Walvoord speaks of God "reviving his people politically" and refers to "the present occupation of Jerusalem," he clearly sees the State of Israel and its capture of East Jerusalem in 1967 as fulfillments of Daniels' prophecies. But if the creation of a Jewish state was a vital part of God's plan for the future, it is hard to see how this could ever be related to Daniel's vision of the coming of the kingdom of God, and in particular to his vision of the Son of Man in chapter 7. Baldwin suggests that this chapter is the climax

---

5. Chapman, *Christian Zionism and the Restoration of Israel*.
6. See further III.9.

of the first half of the book, and that "it is the high point in relation to the whole book."[7]

This vision describes four kingdoms/states (Babylon, Media, Persia, and Greece). What follows the fall of these kingdoms is not another kingdom/state, but the coming of the kingdom of God. We can hardly fail to notice the deliberate contrast between these four kingdoms, which are represented by animals—wild beasts—and a new kind of kingdom, which is represented by a human being (the Son of Man). What comes after the four kingdoms is a community of people which is described as "the holy ones of the Most High," "the people of the holy ones of the Most High" (7:25, 27). This community is made up of "all peoples, nations and languages" (7:14) It is therefore a completely different kind of community, totally different from any political entity, since it will be "an everlasting community" (7:27). If this is what the coming of the kingdom of God would mean, it is hard to understand how a vital part of this kingdom would be the creation of a Jewish state.

If Daniel, therefore, was not looking forward to the creation of the State of Israel, how are we to understand the history that has led to the creation of this state? We need to take time to study the history of the whole Zionist enterprise and the roots of the conflict between Zionist Jews and Palestinian Arabs. The indigenous Jewish communities in Palestine at the beginning of the Zionist movement in the 1880s were no more than 5 percent of the total population. So when the Arabs realized that the Jewish settlers wanted to increase in number and establish a Jewish homeland, or even a Jewish state, it was inevitable that there would be conflict between the two communities. As we study the history of the conflict, we will want to make the same kind of moral judgments that we make about other historical events. We should also judge the State of Israel (and the Palestinians) by the moral standards that we find in the law and the prophets in the Old Testament and by widely accepted principles of human rights and international law. We will therefore want to pray and work for a just and peaceful resolution to the conflict which enables all the people in the land to live in security and enjoy equal

---

7. Baldwin, *Daniel*, 152.

Daniel's prophecies have begun to be fulfilled

rights. Studying history and biblical interpretation side by side in this way may offer a more convincing and fruitful way of understanding what has been happening and continues to happen before our eyes in the Middle East.

Can we therefore conclude that

- if Daniel's visions (including the numbers) were never intended to be interpreted literally;
- if the church is a continuation of Israel and not completely separate from Israel;
- if Daniel's visions of the coming the kingdom of God were not looking forward to a literal millennium, but to the coming of Jesus;
- if the millennium described in Revelation is not a literal period of a thousand years when Jesus will reign from Jerusalem;
- if Daniel's fourth beast is Greece, and can't be a description of a revived Roman Empire in the end times;
- if Daniel was looking forward to a restored temple after the exile and a few centuries later, but not a restored temple in the twentieth century;
- if "the abomination of desolation" represented primarily what Antiochus was doing to the temple in Jerusalem;
- and if Daniel was not describing details of Middle East history in the nineteenth and twentieth centuries;

can dispensationalists be open to consider the alternative way of interpreting Daniel offered in Part I? And perhaps at some stage we need to put the controversy about dispensationalism aside and explore in Part III what positive message Daniel might have for Christians today.

PART III

What Is the Message of Daniel for Today?

Introduction

In Part I we looked at the two possible contexts in which the book was written—Babylon in the sixth century BC and/or Palestine in the second century BC—and explored some of the questions about how the book should be interpreted.

In Part II we examined the basis for the dispensationalist interpretation, which sees the book as a preview of history right up to the second coming of Christ and the beginning of his millennial reign on earth. We challenged this interpretation on the basis of our study in Part I, which concluded that, although the visions look forward to the coming of the kingdom of God, their main focus is on the end of the severe persecution that the Jews were suffering under Antiochus between 167 and 164 BC.

In Part III we ask what Christians today in all their different situations in different parts of the world can learn from the book. Is there a message of encouragement and hope for the future? Is there anything we can learn about the sovereignty of God in history at a time when there is so much conflict? If, after a Bible

Part III: What Is the Message of Daniel for Today?

reading in church we say "This is the word of the Lord," what can God be saying to us today through this book?

Each short chapter ends with questions to stimulate personal reflection or group discussion.

1

Daniel is a model for believers who engage with their context and their culture without compromising their faith

Daniel was probably a young man in 605 BC when he was taken with other Jewish exiles from Jerusalem to Babylon on the first occasion that Nebuchadnezzar besieged the city. He worked in the heart of government in Babylon under four different kings, and saw the Babylonian empire defeated by Cyrus. Early in his time he must have known of Jeremiah's letter to the exiles in which he had encouraged them to settle in Babylon: "Build houses and live in them; plant gardens and eat what they produce.... But seek the welfare of the city where I have sent you into exile, and pray to the LORD on its behalf, for in its welfare you will find your welfare" (Jer 29:4–7). When Cyrus came to power in Babylon in 538 BC and allowed some of the Judean exiles to return to Jerusalem, Daniel didn't return with them, and must have remained in Babylon. He would have been in his eighties in 537 BC, the "third year of King Cyrus of Persia" (10:1), when, according to 11:1 he received the last vision recorded in the book. He therefore remained in Babylon during the whole of the exile.

His gifts and potential were clearly recognized by officials in the king's palace, since he was picked out to "serve in the king's

PART III: WHAT IS THE MESSAGE OF DANIEL FOR TODAY?

palace," along with other "young men without physical defect and handsome, versed in every branch of wisdom, endowed with knowledge and insight" (1:4). Their education involved being taught "the literature and language of the Chaldeans" (1:4), which would mean a total immersion in Babylonian history, culture, and religion. He and his colleagues were given new names, which, according to Lucas, "probably, directly or by implication, invoke Babylonian gods."[1] Taking on new names was no doubt meant to "symbolize becoming good Babylonians."[2]

How then did this approach work out in practice? "Their policy," says Wallace, "was to co-operate, but without compromise.... They readily take on top jobs in the pagan imperial administration."[3] After they have proved their physical fitness, "the palace master brought them into the presence of Nebuchadnezzar, and the king spoke with them. And among them all, no one was found to compare with Daniel, Hananiah, Mishael, and Azariah; therefore they were stationed in the king's court" (1:19). After Daniel interpreted Nebuchadnezzar's dream, he was given rapid promotion: "Then the king promoted Daniel ... and made him ruler over the whole province of Babylon and chief prefect over all the wise men of Babylon" (2:48). He was therefore in effect the head of the civil service. In his top position at the king's court, he must been aware of what was happening within the country and in neighboring countries. Readers today need perhaps to be reminded that Daniel was neither a priest nor a prophet, but a layman who remained in the corridors of power in this foreign country for at least sixty years. But in spite of all the pressures to conform, he found ways to continue with his work in government and at the same time to remain faithful to Israel's God.

How in this situation were Daniel and his colleagues able to remain faithful? If they belonged to a "conquered people in exile,"[4]

1. Lucas, *Daniel*, 53.
2. Lucas, *Daniel*, 57.
3. Wallace, *Lord Is King*, 39.
4. Lucas, *Daniel*, 56.

how in this context were they to hold onto their identity as God-fearing Judeans?

There were two particular issues over which they felt they had to take a stand. "Daniel resolved that he would not defile himself with the royal rations of food and wine" (1:8). It's not clear, however, why he believed that eating the king's food would amount to defilement. Was it because he understood that the food had been offered in the temple to a foreign god, or because it had not been handled in accordance with the Mosaic law? Or was it because eating the king's food implied total allegiance to the king? It could have been a mixture of all these reasons. But there is no suggestion that Daniel continued to live on the same vegetarian diet for the rest of his working life, since we are told concerning a later occasion when he decided to fast: "I had eaten no rich food, no meat or wine had entered my mouth, and I had not anointed myself at all, for the full three weeks" (10:3).

The second issue arose over Nebuchadnezzar's determination that all his subjects should "fall down and worship the golden statue" that he erected. Whether or not this was a statue of himself or some Babylonian god, Wallace suggests that Nebuchadnezzar could have interpreted his earlier dream as a warning about "the lack of cohesion in the society he was re-structuring." He must think that "to develop and unify culture . . . he requires a unifying religion. . . . What better and more lasting cement could there be than a common religion, and a culture deeply influenced by such a common religion?"[5] Daniel's three colleagues—Shadrach, Meshach, and Abednego—must have understood that their loyalty to God must take precedence over their loyalty to the state, and when they refused to bow down to the statue, they were prepared to be thrown into the fiery furnace.

Daniel and his colleagues therefore found a way to be at home in a foreign country and a foreign culture. They were forced to draw a line on two specific issues. But they adapted to their new situation without losing their original identity or assimilating completely to a new culture.

5. Wallace, *Lord Is King*, 63.

Part III: What Is the Message of Daniel for Today?

Questions

1. If Daniel felt that he was living in a foreign country with a very different culture, might Christians in many contexts today feel that they are a tiny minority living in a culture that is very foreign to them? In what ways might they sometimes feel that they are a minority in exile?

2. If Daniel was able to enter into Babylonian culture and understand it fully without adopting its worldview, is it possible for Christians to enter fully into their culture while retaining their Christian worldview?

3. If Daniel and his colleagues chose food as an area where they felt they had to draw a line and make a statement about their identity, what are some of the areas where Christians may need to do draw a line in their different contexts today?

4. If Nebuchadnezzar was attempting to create a unifying religion for all his subjects, can we see similar attempts in past history or at the present time to create a unifying religion? If Nazism was an ideology intended to create a united Germany, are there other dangerous nationalisms in different countries today?

2

God is Sovereign Lord of history; but human beings are still responsible for their actions

We have seen in Part I that one of the basic themes in the book of Daniel is the sovereignty of God in history. Some commentators believe that the visions cover the whole course of human history to the very end. Baldwin, for example writes: "By the use of dreams and visions, signs, symbols, and numbers it appears to be declaring the course of history, and to be drawing attention to the significance of history, by mapping out its course as it proceeds towards its end."[1] Others argue that, while the writer or writers see God as the Lord of all history, their main focus is on the period between the sixth century and the second century BC. All, however, agree over the basic message: God is not only at work in history, but is working towards the goal of establishing his kingly rule in the world.

Alexander Di Lella sums up the implications of this understanding of the sovereignty of God in history:

> The Book of Daniel teaches unambiguously that the God of Israel is the Lord of history and King of all peoples and nations. "The Most High has dominion over man's kingdom, and . . . he gives it to whom he wishes" (4:22).

---

1. Baldwin, *Daniel*, 15.

Part III: What Is the Message of Daniel for Today?

> Everything in time and place forms part of the divine plan, mysterious though it many appear even to the convinced believer. Nothing merely happens. In Dan 1:2, it is the Lord who handed King Jehoiakim of Judah over to Nebuchadnezzar of Babylon. The latter's military might and prowess were simply the instruments God used for his own purposes. Even the arch-villain Antiochus IV Epiphanes ruled over and suppressed the Chosen People only by tacit divine permission (Dan 8:23–26; 9:26–27). Simplistic as these assertions may appear to the sophisticated reader today, they nevertheless convey a calm and serene assurance that history is not an often cruel and haphazard succession of fundamentally meaningless events in which the weak and the poor turn out to be the inevitable victims, but is rather a mysterious unfolding of a plan in which the will of a concerned and loving God will ultimately prevail regardless of the obstinacy and pride of sinful men and women.[2]

> This kind of faith-life may not in every case bring dazzling success as in the charming stories of Daniel 1–6, but it will give the believer a deep and abiding sense of what it means to be a person fashioned in the image of God who is involved in human history and misery and who has given men and women a share in his dominion over the world.[3]

After his painful experience of a mental breakdown, Nebuchadnezzar acknowledges that there is a power in the universe that is greater than himself: "I blessed the Most High, and praised and honored the one who lives for ever. For his sovereignty is an everlasting sovereignty, and his kingdom endures from generation to generation. All the inhabitants of the earth are accounted as nothing, and he does what he wills with the host of heaven and the inhabitants of the earth" (4:34). The message of all the visions in the book is that history is not meaningless, and that God is somehow at

---

2. Di Lella, *Daniel*, 108.
3. Di Lella, *Daniel*, 109–10.

God is Sovereign Lord of history

work in the rise and fall of nations. "God is actually at work in some way," says Lucas, "even in the seemingly chaotic forces of history."[4]

This conviction is often expressed by using the word "control." Baldwin, for example, writes: "The God who initiated human life controls history."[5] Goldingay similarly writes "As the One who controls history, God has insight into history; as the One who has insight into history, God can reveal its significance; as the One who actually can reveal the significance of history, God is proved to be the One who controls history (2:20–23)."[6]

This can be misleading and unhelpful, however, if it suggests that history is like a machine that can be controlled or that human beings are like puppets in the hands of God. There is no suggestion in Daniel that history is pre-determined and that there's no place for human freedom and responsibility. Nebuchadnezzar is challenged by his dream and responds—even if his repentance amounts to a "half-conversion."[7] When Belshazzar sees the writing on the wall, Daniel reminds him that he knew very well the experience of Nebuchadnezzar: "And you, Belshazzar his son, have not humbled your heart, even though you knew all this! You have exalted yourself against the Lord of heaven!" (5:22–23). The Antiochus figure, the "little horn," experiences God's judgment because of his "speaking arrogantly" (7:8), speaking "words against the Most High" (7:25), his "intrigue," "cunning," and "deceit" (8:23–25; 11:21–23), and his determination to crush "the holy ones," "the holy ones of the Most High" (7:21–25).

Commentators like Lucas therefore point out that the book of Daniel recognizes "the tension between belief in God's sovereignty and in human responsibility with which most religious believers are prepared to live in reality, and which is at the heart of the

---

4. Lucas, *Daniel*, 198.
5. Baldwin, *Daniel*, 16.
6. Goldingay, *Daniel*, Word Biblical Themes, 38.
7. Lucas, *Daniel*, 97.

Part III: What Is the Message of Daniel for Today?

experience of prayer."[8] "The tension between divine sovereignty and human responsibility is not lost."[9] He explains further:

> Clearly in the face of rampant evil and great suffering the vision is intended to assure the reader that there is no ultimate dualism. There are evil people and, related to them, spiritual realities that are opposed to God. At times, they seem to be have their way and to be frustrating God's purposes. However, God is sovereign and his purposes will triumph. He is somehow in control even when evil seems to be dominant. Therefore the faithful, and, even more, the waverers, are given encouragement to stand firm and not to throw in their lot with the wicked. Here there is no attempt to resolve the dilemma of affirming God's sovereign control of history while holding to a measure of freedom and responsibility for humans within history. There is an implicit recognition of the tension this produces, and a challenge to live by faith with that tension instead of resolving it by giving way to either fatalism or dualism.[10]

Di Lella describes the kind of answer that Daniel offers to the question of how to reconcile belief in the sovereignty of God with the problem of evil:

> The absolute conviction that God in his time will right all wrongs does not necessarily remove or alleviate the believer's distress in day-to-day living and coping with suffering and sudden death in an oppressive society. In fact, historical realism makes the believer keenly aware that matters are not always set straight in the present age. The Book of Daniel challenges men and women, therefore, to accept in faith the revealed notion of retribution in the afterlife (2:44; 7:14, 18, 22, 27; 12:1–3). Seen in this light, the problem of evil does not cease to be a problem nor does it become less irksome; but it does become a mystery one can learn to live with and accept when one has a lively and abiding faith in an all-wise and almighty God who can and will save. Accordingly, the

---

8. Lucas, *Daniel*, 253.
9. Lucas, *Daniel*, 139–40.
10. Lucas, *Daniel*, 300.

end and goal of human history are in God's hand, not man's. For the believer the inauguration of the Kingdom of God is unquestionably certain; the timetable, however, is not. . . . For this reason the believer can experience in the present moment of crisis and decision a well-grounded hope in the power of God who cannot and will not remain indifferent to human sin, but will redress all evils and restore balance to an otherwise topsy-turvy and often unjust world.[11]

If Daniel was written in the sixth century BC, the Jewish community in Babylon would have been encouraged by the message that the exile would come to an end. They would also be warned that future generations living in Palestine would experience extreme persecution under a foreign ruler. If the book was written or reached its final form in the second century BC, the Jewish community in Palestine would have been encouraged to be told that their suffering under Antiochus would soon come to a end. In both situations they would have been assured that the God who had entered into a covenant relationship with his people was at work in all the inexplicable events that were happening around them. And alongside their confidence in the God of the covenant, they were encouraged to be aware of their own responsibility for the way they responded.

Questions

1. Is it appropriate to use the word "control" to describe God's sovereignty over history? What is the positive message that is conveyed by this word, and what are some of the dangers?

2. How easy do you find it to hold together God's sovereignty in history and human responsibility?

3. How does belief in the sovereignty of God help in facing all the uncertainties and tragedies of life?

---

11. Di Lella, *Daniel*, 106–7.

3

Prayer is a vital way of cooperating with God

There are three particular instances in the book that illustrate the role of prayer in the life of Daniel. Firstly, when Nebuchadnezzar threatens to kill all his advisers because they are unable to tell him his dream and its interpretation, Daniel tells his three colleagues "to seek mercy from the God of heaven concerning this mystery" (2:18). In response to these prayers we're told, "Then the mystery was revealed to Daniel in a vision of the night" (2:17–19). Prayer plays an important role in the remarkable insight and discernment that he demonstrates throughout his life. This insight enables him to understand what is happening in the kingdom of Babylon and the surrounding nations, and to understand from his Scriptures how God is at work in the world and what he is planning to do.

Secondly, when Daniel realizes that he's about to be thrown into the den of lions for disobeying the king's edict about praying to any god other than the king himself, we're told that "he *continued* to go to his house, which had windows in its upper room open toward Jerusalem, and to get down on his knees *three times a day* to pray to his God and praise him, *just as he had done previously*" (6:10). A regular pattern of prayer must have been the backbone of Daniel's spiritual life, and in facing in the direction of Jerusalem he was no doubt aware of Solomon's prayer at the dedication of the temple: "Hear the pleas of your servant and of your people Israel

Prayer is a vital way of cooperating with God

when they pray towards this place; O hear in heaven your dwelling place; heed and forgive" (1 Kgs 8:30). If Solomon in his prayer had spoken of the temple in Jerusalem as "the place of which you said, 'My Name shall be there'" (1 Kgs 8:29), Daniel knew that all his prayers were based on his understanding of the temple as the symbol of God's desire to live among his people.

The third occasion is Daniel's prayer in which he pleads for God to honor his commitment to restore the people to the land after their seventy years of exile: "Then I turned to the Lord God, to seek an answer by prayer and supplication with fasting and sackcloth and ashes. I prayed to the LORD my God and made confession, saying . . ." (9:3-4). Goldingay writes that this prayer "arises out of the reading of Scripture, and illustrates the interplay there can be between the words of Scripture and the words of prayer, as Scripture stimulates prayer and prayer forms the appropriate response to Scripture."[1] Daniel therefore confesses the sins of his people, which have led to the exile, and prays for restoration to the land and the restoration of Jerusalem and its temple (9:4-19). His plea can only be based "on the ground of your great mercies," and on his conviction that "your city and your people bear your name" (9:18-19). In response to his prayer Gabriel tells him "I have now come out to give you wisdom and understanding" (9:20-23). The understanding that he gives to Daniel in the following verses (9:24-27) concerns not only the return from exile but a great deliverance that is to come in a future generation.[2]

If we ask about the content of Daniel's prayers, "They are prayers," says Goldingay, "which involve petition, intercession, confession, and thanksgiving."[3] In his petition Daniel is asking for insight to interpret a dream and for deliverance from the den of lions. In his intercession he is pleading for the restoration of his people to the land and the restoration of the temple. His confession recognizes the seriousness of his people's sin over many years: "We have sinned and done wrong, acted wickedly and rebelled,

---

1. Goldingay, *Daniel*, Word Biblical Themes, 52-53.
2. See further I.6.
3. Goldingay, *Daniel*, Word Biblical Themes, 45.

turning aside from your commandments and ordinances. We have not listened to your servants the prophets. . . . [W]e have sinned against you. . . . All Israel has transgressed your law and turned aside, refusing to obey your voice" (9:4–14). His thanksgiving is prompted first by the way God has answered his prayer by revealing Nebuchadnezzar's dream and its interpretation. He blesses the God of heaven because "wisdom and power are his," and because this same God has also given "wisdom and power" to Daniel (2:19–23). Later in his prayer for the restoration of his people, Daniel addresses Yahweh as the "great and awesome God, keeping covenant and steadfast love with those who love you" (9:3) and as the God "who brought your people out of the land of Egypt with a mighty hand and made your name renowned even to this day" (9:15).

What role, therefore, does Daniel's prayer play in the whole story? It seems that his prayer is not only a way of presenting his petitions to God, but is a way of cooperating with God in getting his will done in the world. He understands that God, as the God of the covenant, has promised to bring his people back to their land after repentance, and he wants to be working with God to bring this about. Goldingay relates this idea to the words in Isaiah where God says "Before they call I will answer":

> The point expressed in loving hyperbole in Isa. 65:24 (cf. 65:1) here becomes prosaic narrative reality: God is so eager to respond to prayer (and the divine sovereignty in human affairs is so real) that the response comes before the prayer is actually over (9:20, 21). The prayer offered the response to God's prophetic word which made the fulfilment of that word possible. The promise of fulfillment issues when Daniel turns to God, yet it issues before he actually prays his lament, so that the story affirms not only the importance of prayer and the place it has in the outworking of God's purpose (it is in response to prayer that God acts) but also the importance of God's sovereignty (prayer is a means of God's good will being put into effect). One person's prayer brings about

the restoration of the people of God; but it is a matter of releasing that restoration which God has already purposed.[4]

Towards the end of the book Daniel becomes aware that, through his prayers and all his activity on behalf of his people, he is somehow involved in an ongoing spiritual conflict in the heavenly world. We have already seen (in I.8) that when Paul writes about "our struggle . . . against the rulers, against the authorities, against the cosmic powers of this present darkness" (Eph 6:12), he may be thinking of Daniel's description of conflict in the heavenly world. Wallace writes:

> Daniel himself, in his sensitivity to what was going on in the other realm, was caught up into this conflict, was able to participate in it through his prayers, and thus to help to bring about sooner the successful outcome. . . . It is thus asserted that in the heavenly sphere there is some kind of participation in the conflicts and troubles of earth; and in the earthly sphere, especially through the intercession of the people of God, there can be some kind of participation in working out of destiny on a much more cosmic scale than if often understood.[5]

Questions

1. If Daniel's prayer includes petition and intercession, confession and thanksgiving, does this suggest that our prayer should also contain all these elements?

2. If Daniel understood what God was wanting to do and through his prayer was cooperating with God in getting his will done, can this help us to understand what we are doing when we pray "Your will be done"?

---

4. Goldingay, *Daniel*, 49–50.
5. Wallace, *Lord Is King*, 179–80.

4

God's people need to learn how to live in different political contexts

We have seen in Part I that, if the whole book of Daniel was written in the sixth century BC, it was predicting events that would take place in Palestine in the second century BC. If, however, it was put together in its final form in the second century BC, it could have been using material from an earlier period and adding new material in order to give an interpretation of the intense suffering the Jewish community were experiencing under Antiochus Epiphanes. These two different contexts are separated by many hundreds of miles and around four hundred years.

The stories about Daniel in Babylon in chapters 1–6 come from a context in which the Jewish people are exiles in a foreign land. They are a minority, but a tolerated minority. They have been taken to Babylon along with leaders of the community in Jerusalem, but they are not suffering any kind of ongoing persecution. Daniel and his companions—Hananiah, Mishael, and Azariah—are selected for work in the king's palace, and are put through a rigorous programme of training in which they have to study the history, culture, politics, and religion of Babylon. When they are later interviewed by Nebuchadnezzar himself and seen to be "better than all the magicians and enchanters in his whole kingdom,"

God's people need to learn how to live in different political contexts

they are all "stationed in the king's court" (1:18–20). After Daniel interprets the king's dream, Nebuchadnezzar promotes him and makes him "ruler over the whole province of Babylon and chief prefect over all the wise men of Babylon," and he remains in this position under several different kings for around sixty years "until the first year of King Cyrus" (1:21). In the words of Baldwin, therefore, "Daniel and his friends represent the followers of the living God at the courts of the most powerful rulers the world had yet seen."[1]

Their faith and their commitment, however, are severely tested. Daniel's three companions are thrown into the fiery furnace because of their refusal to worship Nebuchadnezzar's golden statue; but after their rescue, they are promoted "in the province of Babylon" (3:1–30). Daniel is thrown into the den of lions because of his refusal to pray to Darius, the king; but after his rescue, we are told that "he prospered during the reign of Darius and the reign of Cyrus the Persian" (6:28). These Jewish exiles have therefore have been thoroughly integrated into a foreign culture. But when their faith is severely tested, they remain faithful to the God of Israel and are able to continue their work in the government of the country.

The situation faced by the Jewish communities in Palestine in the second century under Antiochus could hardly be more different from the situation of the communities in Babylon in the sixth century. Writing about the visions in chapters 7–11, Goldingay comments, "The visions presuppose a setting in Jerusalem in the 160s where power lies in the hands of constitutionally hostile gentile authorities and a compliant Jewish leadership that has cooperated with the subversion and outlawing of traditional Jewish faith. . . . [The] authors and audience seem to be people who feel ousted from power in their community, which is divided into people who support the foreign government and people who oppose it. They are persecuted by these foreign overlords and puzzled at their God's failure to act in response to attacks on his sphere—his sanctuary, its priesthood, its worship, its people."[2]

1. Baldwin, *Daniel* 148.
2. Goldingay, *Daniel*, 577–79.

Part III: What Is the Message of Daniel for Today?

This situation comes about because Antiochus' attempt to suppress the Jewish religion "precipitated the greatest crisis in the history of the Judahites between the fall of Jerusalem in 586 and the event of the first century AD."[3] We have already seen (in I.1) how the detailed accounts in 1 and 2 Maccabees of the measures that Antiochus takes—like the banning of Sabbath observance and circumcision, the destruction of the books of the law, and the erection of an altar to Zeus in the temple—are reflected in Daniel's dreams in chapters 7, 8, 9, and 11. These measures have divided the Jewish community, with one party willing to accept Antiochus' programme of Hellenization, and others vigorously resisting, and even facing death for continuing to circumcise their children.

How is it possible that a writer or writers in the sixth century could predict with such accuracy a totally different situation which their people would face four hundred years later in Palestine? Or why would writers in the second century use stories from earlier centuries that reflected a very different political context? These questions about the different ethos of the two parts of Daniel have been discussed endlessly in discussions about the authorship and date of the book. So is it possible to suggest how a single writer or group of writers could have put the book together in its present form?

The suggestion outlined in I.10 is that one or more writers in the 160s BC brought together traditional stories about Daniel in Babylon that had been handed down for many generations, and, by describing a series of visions which they attributed to Daniel, added their own interpretation of the events through which they were living in Palestine. Both in Babylon and in Palestine the Jewish community faced real dilemmas and challenges: How could they remain faithful to their God when their rulers were demanding unquestioning allegiance? Were they prepared for martyrdom if they were not prepared to submit? Lucas explains how a book that reflects two very different situations can still communicate a single coherent message:

---

3. Goldingay, *Daniel*, 390.

God's people need to learn how to live in different political contexts

> This linking back of the visions to the stories through ch. 7 tells us that the difference of ethos in the two parts of the book does not come from contradictory worldviews. Rather, it represents two ends of the spectrum of the experience of the godly person living in a pagan society. Sometimes it is possible to be both faithful to one's principles and fully involved in the society. At other times, the society can be so hostile that the principles are trampled on, and the godly may be crushed. This parallels the difference in ethos between Paul's positive view of the Roman government in Rom. 13 and John's negative view of it in Rev. 13. Both situations present challenges and temptations to test the faithfulness of those seeking to remain true to their vision of God.[4]

One of the basic messages of the book, therefore, can be summed up in this way: The people of God need to be prepared to live in very different—and very difficult—political situations. When they are a tolerated minority, there will be some issues where they will have to draw certain lines if they want to remain faithful to their God. When they are being suppressed as a persecuted minority, they can trust that history is not out of control. When they don't experience a miraculous deliverance, they can be assured that their persecutors will ultimately be judged by the Sovereign Lord of history, and that they will experience vindication beyond the grave.

It's not surprising to learn that the book of Daniel has conveyed a powerful message to Christians who have been suffering. Newsom describes how Korean Christians understood the book of Daniel as they lived under oppressive Japanese rule:

> One can find examples of Daniel's legacy of subtle resistance even in recent times. During the Imperial Japanese occupation of Korea in the early twentieth century, the Japanese practices of imposing the Japanese language, renaming Koreans with Japanese names, and forcing worship at Shinto shrines seemed to some Korean Christians to parallel the Babylonian practices of Daniel

---

4. Lucas, *Daniel*, 195.

Part III: What Is the Message of Daniel for Today?

1:1–7. In response, Korean Christians told the stories in the books of Daniel and Exodus to encourage resistance to perceived idolatry and the hope for both survival and eventual deliverance. As a Western missionary described the situation, "Neither the preacher nor the teacher would speak directly about the Korean people under the Japanese rule. They only spoke of the people of Israel. . . . Not surprisingly, the Old Testament and more particularly the book of Exodus and the book of Daniel were most disliked by the Japanese authorities and later banned from the church." Fifty years later, a group of South African theologians produced the Kairos Document, a theological rejection of the apartheid regime and a call for resistance that highlights the importance of civil disobedience, citing (among other texts) the book of Daniel as a scriptural example of such action, emphasizing Dan 1.[5]

Questions

1. There can't be any situations in the world that are comparable to the Christendom that existed in Europe for many centuries. But can we see any similarities between the situation of Daniel in Babylon in the sixth century and the situation of Christian communities in many countries today where they are a tiny, powerless minority?

2. Can we see similarities between the situation of Jewish communities in Palestine under the rule of Antiochus in Palestine in the second century and the situation of Christian communities suffering today under rulers who are trying to suppress them and their faith? What is the message of Daniel for Christians who are persecuted by the state?

3. Daniel would have had a much more positive attitude towards the different kings under whom he worked than the communities in Palestine would have had towards Antiochus. Does

5. Newsom, *Daniel*, 56–57.

God's people need to learn how to live in different political contexts

this help us to understand why Paul in Romans 13:1–7 could have a positive view of Roman imperial authority, while for John in Revelation 13 Rome is symbolized by "the beast"?

5

While God sometimes delivers his people in miraculous ways, at other times they have to face persecution and suffering

The stories about Daniel and his companions in children's Bibles focus on the miraculous deliverances—the three men from the fiery furnace in chapter 3 and Daniel from the lions' den in chapter 6. But they don't have anything to say about the persecution and suffering of the people of God, which is a major theme in the visions in the second half of the book. One of the most striking features of the book, therefore, is the differences between the two halves of the book.

In the first deliverance story, it is clear from the way the three companions respond to the king that they believe that God is able to deliver them if he chooses to do so, but that they cannot take it for granted that God will deliver them: "O Nebuchadnezzar, . . . [i]f our God whom we serve is able to deliver us from the furnace of blazing fire and out of your hand, O king, let him deliver us. But if not, be it known to you, O king, that we will not serve your gods and we will not worship the golden statue that you have set up" (3:16–18). They have complete confidence in their God and are willing to accept however God responds to the real threat of death.

> While God sometimes delivers his people in miraculous ways

Many readers today will wonder whether the story is to be understood literally. Commentators have pointed out the irony and even humor with which the story is told.[1] Baldwin writes that

> The majority of commentators regard this chapter [chapter 3] as a kind of allegory rather than as a historical event. Every aspect of the story has in turn been called in question, but evidence has been produced to establish the realism of its features, strange as they are to the modern western reader.... Thus there is nothing improbable about the story until it comes to the miraculous intervention by which the lives of the three men were saved and a fourth accompanied them in the furnace.[2]

Others, however, question whether the writer intended the story to be understood literally. Goldingday, for example, writes:

> Did the story happen? I don't know. I'm inclined to assume that farces are more likely to be fictional than factual. Like the young men, I know that God can miraculously rescue people from their persecutors. God has many aides whom he can send to deliver people from red-hot furnaces of one kind and another. But I also know that he usually doesn't do so, and the story offers no promise that he'll do so for other people put in the position of these three youths. So it doesn't make a lot of difference whether it happened or not. It probably won't happen for us. The story constitutes an encouragement to live by the principles they enunciated to Nebuchadnezzar, or the principle embodied in the rabbis who find God guilty and then break off to say their prayers.[3]

If the stories in the first half of the book are about miraculous deliverance, the visions in the second half reflect the suffering of God's people. We have already seen (in I.8), that there are several passages in the visions that speak of the intense persecution that the people are going to suffer:

1. Goldingay, *Daniel and the Twelve Prophets for Everyone*, 21.
2. Baldwin, *Daniel*, 111–12.
3. Goldingay, *Daniel and the Twelve Prophets for Everyone*, 21.

PART III: WHAT IS THE MESSAGE OF DANIEL FOR TODAY?

- "This horn made war with the holy ones and was prevailing over them" (Dan 7:21)
- "He . . . shall wear out the holy ones of the Most High . . . and they shall be given into his power" (7:25)
- "They shall fall by the sword and flame, and suffer captivity and plunder" (Dan 11:33)
- "There shall be a time of anguish, such as has never occurred since nations first came into existence" (12:1)
- "When the shattering of the power of the holy people comes to an end . . ." (12:7)

We have also noted that, whether scholars believe the book was written in the sixth or second centuries BC, they are unanimous in believing that the persecution that is described in these verses reflects accurately the experience of the Jewish people under Antiochus that is described in great detail in 1 and 2 Maccabees. Commentators are therefore challenged to explain how a single writer or a group of writers would ever put stories of miraculous deliverance alongside predictions of severe persecution. This is how three different commentators deal with this question:

> *[Baldwin:]* Daniel and his friends had been delivered by unusual divine interventions from death, but the warning here is that this will not always be the case. *Sword and flame, captivity and plunder* sum up the sufferings of faithful men and women to this day.[4]

> *[Goldingay:]* It is all very well for earlier chapters of the book to tell stories about God rescuing people from the fire and the lion pit, but more often the fire and the lions have devoured the martyrs. The stories in Daniel affirm that occasional experiences of the faithful God intervening on Israel's behalf are more important than the regular experience of God's non-intervention. . . .
>
> The visions in Daniel, and particularly chapters 10–12, encourage us to look for deliverance after death if

---

4. Baldwin, *Daniel*, 217.

While God sometimes delivers his people in miraculous ways not before it, and Christ's resurrection is for us the guarantee that such deliverance is not mere fanciful hope. "It was the same God of the three youth who was the God of the Maccabees. The former escaped fire, the latter were executed by fires, but both will conquer in the eternal God" (Augustine, *Expositions on the Book of Psalms*).[5]

[Lucas:] The fact is that, down the centuries, God's people have drawn strength from these stories by applying them to their own situations of tribulation, not by focusing on the miraculous deliverances, but by focusing on the steadfastness of Daniel and his three friends in their refusal to deny their faith in God and their commitment to him. The evidence indicates that we have the book of Daniel in its present form because faithful Jews drew great strength from it during the attempt of Antiochus IV Epiphanes to stamp out the Jewish faith. . . .

The persecuted Anabaptists of the sixteenth century quoted from or alluded to the book of Daniel more than to any other biblical book to sustain themselves and others in their struggle. The striking thing is that what they appeal to is not the hope of miraculous deliverance *from* death, such as described in [Daniel] chs. 3 and 6, but the example of the faithful courage of the three young men in ch. 3 and Daniel in ch. 6, and the promise to "the wise" in 12:1–4 that they will be delivered *through* death to everlasting life with God.[6]

Questions

1. In situations of real danger, it's natural for us to pray for protection and deliverance. It would be unbelief on our part if we don't believe that God is able to deliver us. But it will be presumption if we assume that God is certain to deliver us. How then do we avoid both unbelief and presumption?

---

5. Goldingay, *Daniel*, Word Biblical Themes, 20.
6. Lucas, *Daniel*, 155, 305.

PART III: WHAT IS THE MESSAGE OF DANIEL FOR TODAY?

2. The visions offer the assurance that if the people of God are not delivered from suffering in this life, they will vindicated beyond death. How can this kind of assurance help Christians today who are suffering for their faith?

6

God has his own ways into the hearts of authoritarian rulers

In the stories in the first half of the book, Nebuchadnezzar and Belshazzar are the two most significant rulers, and there are very obvious differences in the way they relate to Daniel and his God.

Nebuchadnezzar appears at the very beginning of Daniel, where we're told that he besieged Jerusalem, took "some of the vessels of the house of God," and placed them "in the treasury of his gods." But this is not seen as an accident of history, because we're told that "The Lord let King Jehoiakim of Judah fall into his power" (1:1–2). Nothing critical is said about Nebuchadnezzar at this stage of the story, and he is the one who recruits Daniel and his colleagues to work in his civil service.

When Daniel's dream is interpreted, Nebuchadnezzar acknowledges the superior powers of Daniel's God: "Truly, your God is God of gods and Lord of kings and a revealer of mysteries, for you have been able to reveal this mystery" (2:47). After this confession, things begin to go wrong when he sets up a statue and demands that all his subjects "fall down and worship the golden statue that King Nebuchadnezzaar has set up" (3:5). When Daniel's three friends are delivered from the fiery furnace, Nebuchadnezzar makes another confession about their God:

Part III: What Is the Message of Daniel for Today?

> Blessed be the God of Shadrach, Meshach, and Abednego, who has sent his angel and delivered his servants who trusted in him. They disobeyed the king's command and yielded up their bodies rather than serve and worship any god except their own God. . . . His kingdom is an everlasting kingdom, and his sovereignty is from generation to generation. (3:28; 4:3)

He is beginning to recognize that there is something unique about the God of these Jewish exiles.

Nebuchadnezzar's second dream leads to a crisis, but marks another turning point. Through the dream, says Daniel, God is telling Nebuchadnezzar that he will experience a complete mental breakdown until he has "learned that the Most High has sovereignty over the kingdom of mortals, and gives it to whom he will" (4:25). This is what begins to unfold the moment after he expresses his pride over all his achievements in Babylon: "Is this not magnificent Babylon, which I have built as a royal capital by my mighty power and for my glorious majesty?" (4:30). William Blake's memorable etching portrays the state in which he finds himself: "He was driven away from human society, ate grass like oxen, and his body was bathed with the dew of heaven, until his hair grew as long as an eagle's feathers and his nails became like birds' claws" (4:33).

God has his own ways into the hearts of authoritarian rulers

The final chapter in the Nebuchadnezzar story tells of his recovery and a deeper recognition of the sovereignty of God:

> When that period was over, I Nebuchadnezzar, lifted my eyes to heaven and my reason returned to me. I blessed the Most High, and praised and honored the one who lives forever. For his sovereignty is an everlasting sovereignty, and his kingdom endures from generation to generation.... Now I, Nebuchadnezzar, praise and extol and honor the King of heaven, for all his works are truth, and his ways are justice; and he is able to bring low those who walk in pride. (4:34–37)

As a result of his change of mind, he says, "I was re-established over my kingdom, and still more greatness was added to me" (4:36).

Does his change of mind amount to a personal commitment to Daniel's God? Lucas writes that "Since the king has accepted that God rules *over* him, it is now possible for God to rule *through* him, and so he is restored to his kingdom and greatness."[1] He concludes, however, that "the king is only 'half-converted' in the end."[2] Baldwin comes to the same conclusion: "This impersonal reference to God keeps him at a distance, and this last word of Nebuchadnezzar in the book, while formally acknowledging the power and justice of God, appears to fall short of penitence and true faith."[3]

The story of Belshazzar, who comes to the throne after Nebuchadnezzar, is much shorter and doesn't have such a positive conclusion. A single chapter tells the story of "a great festival for a thousand of his lords" (5:1), in which Belshazzar commands "that they bring in the vessels of gold and silver that his father Nebuchadnezzar had taken out of the temple in Jerusalem so that the king and his lords, his wives and his concubines might drink from them.... They drank wine and praised the gods of gold and silver, bronze, iron, wood and stone" (5:2–4). In the eyes of Jews who hate idolatry of any kind, Belshazzar's actions amount to "slighting the deity of the God of Israel, the one true God.... Belshazzar is then condemned

---

1. Lucas, *Daniel*, 118.
2. Lucas, *Daniel*, 97.
3. Baldwin, *Daniel*, 129.

for pride that is more culpable than Nebuchadnezzar's because it is not based on any great achievements . . . and he has ignored the lessons of his 'father's' experience."[4] Baldwin describes Belshazzar's banquet as "sheer bravado, the last fling of a terrified ruler unsuccessfully attempting to drown his fears."[5] Similarly Wallace points out the contrast between Belshazzar and Nebuchadnezzar: "We saw Nebuchadnezzar treating the sacred vessels of the God of Israel with respect and decency. We now see Belshazzar using them sacrilegiously only to add a little novelty to his last drunken orgy."[6]

We are told that "Immediately the fingers of a human hand appeared and began writing on the plaster of the wall of the royal palace" (5:5). When the wise men are unable to interpret the meaning of the four words, the queen reminds Belshazzar of Daniel, who had proved to Nebuchadnezzar to be "a man . . . endowed with a spirit of the holy gods" (5:11). Daniel begins his interpretation by retelling the story of Nebuchadnezzar and how "when his heart was lifted up and his spirit was hardened so that he acted proudly," he suffered an extreme breakdown and "was driven from human society . . . until he learned that the Most High God has sovereignty over the kingdom of mortals, and sets over it whosoever he will." Then comes the challenge:

> And you, Belshazzar his son, have not humbled your heart, even though you knew all this! You have exalted yourself against the Lord of heaven! The vessels of his temple have been brought in before you, and you and your lords, your wives and your concubines have been drinking wine from them. You have praised the gods of silver and gold, of bronze, iron, wood, and stone, . . . but the God in whose power is your very breath, and to whom belong all your ways, you have not honored. (5:20–23)

After Daniel explains the meaning of the words on the wall—that "God has numbered the days of your kingdom and brought it to an end" (5:26–28)—"that very night Belshazzar, the Chaldean king, was killed" (5:30).

4. Lucas, *Daniel*, 139.
5. Baldwin, *Daniel*, 133.
6. Wallace, *Lord Is King*, 88.

God has his own ways into the hearts of authoritarian rulers

Both these stories teach that the one Creator God has his own way into the hearts of even the most powerful autocrats in the world. If the whole book of Daniel was written in the sixth century BC, the Jewish community in Babylon would have been encouraged to be reminded that the God of Israel was no mere tribal deity, but the God who is concerned about all the nations of the world—and their rulers. If it reached its final form in the second century BC, the community in Palestine would have understood that the story of God's dealings with Nebuchadnezzar and Belshazzar provided the assurance that their God knew how to deal with a cruel autocrat like Antiochus.

Lucas sees this as a major message in the whole book of Daniel: "Pride, especially the hubris of rulers who think they can 'play god', is a theme that runs through the book of Daniel."[7] Goldingay suggests how we should think of world rulers today when he writes that Daniel

> is not merely a story about a miraculous escape from martyrdom, but about all human claims to sovereign immutability yielding to God's abiding will and about the miracle of the human sovereign himself acknowledging that.[8]

> Daniel encourages us to long for God to have compassion on world rulers, specifically the wicked ones, and he encourages us to believe that judgment is never inevitable. We are to treat people in power as given their responsibility by God. We are to appeal to their humanness, not to bait their sinfulness. The confession of God as king might seem to leave no place for human government. Actually the chapter assumes that if God's kingship is acknowledged, human sovereignty can then find its place. At the end of the story, even the majesty and glory of human kingship are affirmed. Rule on earth as well as the rule of heaven come to belong to the one who is poor in spirit.[9]

---

7. Lucas, *Daniel*, 116.
8. Goldingay, *Daniel*, Word Biblical Themes, 32.
9. Goldingay, *Daniel*, Word Biblical Themes, 27–28.

Part III: What Is the Message of Daniel for Today?

Newsom sees the stories in the first part of the book as a drama in which everything depends of whether these gentile kings recognize the sovereignty of God and see their own sovereignty as a "delegated sovereignty":

> The drama of the stories can be grasped in terms of whether and how the Gentile King will recognize the true nature of eternal divine sovereignty and the actual source of his own, delegated sovereignty. Daniel and his friends enter the various King's courts ostensibly as prisoners who are granted special training so that they may become courtiers and administrative officials. But their most significant role is to be conduits of the power of the Jewish God—the "God of Heaven," the "Most High." The encounter between the power of the Most High and the Gentile Kings will establish that it is actually the God the Jews who is in control of history and who delegates and eventually takes back sovereignty over the earth. How the Gentile Kings learn this lesson is the burden of each of the narratives.[10]

> [T]he book of Daniel as a whole can be characterized as an extended meditation on the relation between divine and human—especially Gentile—sovereignty.[11]

Questions

1. An autocrat has been defined as "a ruler who has absolute power," "a person ruling with unlimited authority." Who do you see as the most significant autocrats in the world today?
2. What can we learn from the ways God interacts with Nebuchadnezzar and Belshazzar?
3. How should we should be praying for the autocrats in the world today?

---

10. Newsom, *Daniel*, 33.
11. Newsom, *Daniel*, 212.

7

Christians need to take the task of biblical interpretation seriously

Daniel is one book of the Bible where it's never enough to say "The Bible says." Those who see the Bible as "the word of God," and have the highest view of the authority and inspiration of Scripture are still faced with questions about how to interpret it and how to understand what this particular book is saying to us today. Having preached about the book and then taught about it in a seminary, Wallace writes: "I really had to face acutely for the first time the academic and pastoral problems of interpreting such a book for today."[1]

If some parts of the Bible are crystal clear and hardly need any interpretation, other parts—including much of Daniel—are much harder to interpret. But if every book of the Bible raises particular questions about how it should be interpreted, what is special about the book of Daniel? What are the special difficulties in interpreting Daniel?

There is a bewildering variety of interpretations of Daniel's visions
It's hard to think of another book of the Bible that has created so much controversy with so many conflicting interpretations. We

---

1. Wallace, *Lord Is King*, 11.

PART III: WHAT IS THE MESSAGE OF DANIEL FOR TODAY?

have already noted (in I.6) that the verse about the "seventy weeks" in 9:24 is probably the most problematic verse in the whole book, and that Montgomery has written that "The history of the exegesis of the 70 Weeks is the Dismal Swamp of O.T. criticism."[2]

It is understandable, therefore, that one response is to sidestep discussion of the critical questions, and concentrate on the central messages of the book. Chris Wright takes this approach in his *Hearing the Message of Daniel: Sustaining Faith in Today's World*:

> This book takes no position on the critical questions of the unity of Daniel, or the dating of its later chapters, or of the book as a whole. Clearly the entire book is intended to be an encouragement to God's people in the midst of hostile and threatening cultures and to affirm God's sovereign control of all that happens, even as fallen human beings "do as they please" in exercising their own rebellious wills in opposition to God and his people. So I have sought to read and expound the book from within its own perspective and from the angle of its own visions. Those who want to explore the scholarly debate over whether the visions of the later chapters are truly predictive or a prophetic interpretation of past and present events need to consult larger commentaries.[3]

The approach adopted in this book is to face the difficult questions and to explain in some detail the reasons for preferring one particular interpretation. As we saw in the Introduction, this was the approach adopted by Calvin in his commentary on Daniel: "I do not usually refer to conflicting opinions, because I take no pleasure in refuting them, and the simple method which I adopt pleases me best, namely, to expound what I think delivered by the Spirit of God."[4] Whichever approach we adopt to the special difficulties with this book, however, no one can afford to be dogmatic about their approach to interpretation. Newsom's commentary on Daniel contains pages after each chapter entitled "History of

---

2. Lucas, *Daniel*, 245–46.
3. Wright, *Hearing the Message of Daniel*, 12.
4. Goldingay, *Daniel*, 482.

Christians need to take the task of biblical interpretation seriously Daniel's Reception," written by Brennan W. Breed. It's a salutary and humbling exercise for any modern commentator to read the wide variety of interpretations that have been offered by Jewish and Christian readers over the centuries, all of which were inevitably influenced by the contexts in which they were written.[5]

It is always important to understand the context or contexts in which any book of the Bible was written, and much of the controversy about the interpretation of Daniel revolves around the question of whether the second half of the book—or the whole book—was written in the sixth or the second centuries BC.

Every commentary on Daniel points out the different contexts of the two halves of the books. The stories in chapters 1–6 are about the community of Jewish exiles in Babylon between the years 605 and 538 BC. The exiles in Babylon are reasonably secure, and Daniel and his companions have prominent positions in government, although their commitment to their faith is severely tested on at least two occasions. The visions in chapters 7–11 reflect later centuries and events that come to a climax in the second century. The community in Palestine in the second century is suffering severe persecution under a ruler who is attempting to stamp out their religion. If these two contexts are so completely different, how could a *single* writer in *one* of these contexts (the sixth century or the second century) have written in the same book about *both* these contexts at the same time?

Wallace argues for a sixth-century date and writes about the context in which the whole book was written and sums up the kind of message that was required in the Babylonian context:

> Throughout the whole book it becomes obvious that the work is written as a message not primarily for those who are suffering in the midst of deadly persecution but rather for those who are living in a settled condition yet within an alien culture—in other words, not a Maccabean-type situation, but in a Babylonian-type situation. . . . Their message is not one of how to live in the last days under

---

5. See the Preface in Newsom, *Daniel,* xii–xiii.

severe tribulation, but one of how to live in settled times, maintaining a sober view of the future possible evil developments, and working so as to prevent if possible such developments. This does not seem to be the type of message or the type of book one would deliberately write for people who had to live through the days of Antiochus.[6]

In this situation what is required is the steady pursuit of the good life as far as the environment will allow it, faithful co-operation with those in authority as far as conscience will permit, strict adherence to the customs of the law in spite of the opposition that might occur, the cultivation of regular habits of devotion, a pride in the nation's religious traditions, and a willingness to listen to others telling their visions and dreams, and taking an active part in political life and even accepting high office.[7]

But what if the stories about Daniel and his companions were written in the sixth century, but then used as the starting point for writing about the new, extremely threatening situation that the Jews were facing in Palestine under Antiochus? In this case a Jew writing in Palestine in the 160s wants to remind his community about the faithfulness of God to his people living in exile in Babylon in earlier centuries, but at the same time show them that their God can be just as faithful to them in their own situation, which is very different. The writer or writers of the later chapters understand fully the differences between the two contexts, and understand that the different contexts require different messages. As they live under Antiochus' severe oppression, they need the assurance that it will come to an end, and that if they have to die for their faith, they will receive vindication beyond the grave. In these circumstances they cannot write with the same freedom that a sixth-century author could have written, and have to encode their message in the form of apocalyptic—in the same way that John does in writing in the book of Revelation about oppression under Rome.

6. Wallace, *Lord Is King*, 21–22.
7. Wallace, *Lord Is King*, 21.

Christians need to take the task of biblical interpretation seriously

Deciding between a sixth-century and a second-century date doesn't depend on our beliefs about the authority and inspiration of the Bible or the possibility of predictive prophecy.

Those who support a sixth-century date often argue that support for the second-century date is based on the conviction that a writer in the sixth century could not possibly predict in such detail what was to happen four centuries later. Walvoord, for example, points out that in the first Christian centuries scholars were unanimous in their belief that the whole of Daniel was written in the sixth century, and that the first person to challenge this view was Porphyry, the non-Christian philosopher in the early fourth century. Porphyry's argument in favor of the second century date was revived by critics in the seventeenth century. Walvoord argues in response to support for a second-century date:

> It should be noted at the outset that (1) the theory has an anti-Christian origination; (2) no new facts were raised that challenged the previous judgment of the church; and (3) the support of Porphyry by higher critics was part of their overall approach to the Scriptures, which tended almost without exception to deny the traditional authorship of most books of the Bible. They claimed that books frequently had several authors and went through many redactions, and—most importantly, included the almost universal denial by the higher critics of the traditional doctrine of biblical inerrancy and verbal, plenary inspiration. The attack on Daniel was part of an attack upon the entire Scriptures, using the historical-critical method.[8]

Two of the most recent commentators on Daniel, however, Goldingay and Lucas, who support the second century date, hold a traditional understanding of the authority and inspiration of Scripture, as Lucas explains:

> For many supporters of a second-century date the possibility of predictive prophecy ("Could God do it?") is not the issue. Rather, there are two other, to them more relevant, issues. One is primarily theological ("Would

---

8. Walvoord, *Daniel*, 21–22.

God do it?") and the other primarily literary-critical ("Did God do it?").

Faced with the fact that all Daniel's visions focus on the time of Antiochus Epiphanes, Collins gives expression to the theological issue: "There is no apparent reason . . . why a prophet of the sixth century should focus such minute attention on the events of the second century." One response to this is to argue that the reason is that, by giving the prediction so far ahead of time, God assures the people of the second century that he is indeed in control of history, including the situation in which they find themselves. One cannot deny that this has some plausibility. However, an evangelical scholar, Goldingay, can argue that this is not consistent with the picture of God revealed elsewhere in Scripture. As he puts it, "He does not give signs and reveal dates. His statements about the future are calls to decision now; he is not the God of prognostications. He calls his people to naked faith and hope in him in the present, and does not generally bolster their faith with the kind of revelations that we are thinking of here. He does sometimes grant evidences to those who cannot believe without them, and thus we dare not exclude the possibility that this was the case with the book of Daniel. But the presumption is by no means in favour of this possibility." The argument here is not conclusive either way. Both Collins and Goldingay appeal to what they see to be the balance of (theological) possibility. Those who conclude otherwise should at least acknowledge that there is theological integrity on both sides of the argument.[9]

Appreciating the particular kind of literary genre of the stories in Daniel chapters 1–6 can help us to understand their message.

Lucas explains that there was a genre of "court tales" which seems to have been quite widespread in ancient Near East and eastern Mediterranean culture:

---

9. Lucas, *Daniel*, 308–9.

Christians need to take the task of biblical interpretation seriously

It was popular because the royal court was seen as an exotic location and successful courtiers had celebrity status. These tales have three major characteristics. They are a form of entertainment and so are carefully crafted tales and make use of humour. They are educative, with a moral message. The "good courtier" is presented as role model to follow and the "bad courtier" and his demise is a warning of how not to behave. Those tales in which the hero is a foreigner often have the aim of encouraging subjugated people to maintain their ethnic identity, with its culture and religion. Seeing Dan. 1–6 in this context suggests it is a mistake to assume that they can be read like modern historical biographies. They need to be appreciated for what they are and what the author is seeking to do in telling the story. Post-colonial interpreters have noted how humour, especially satire, is used to lampoon the king and the courtiers opposed to Daniel, and how this serves to subvert the imperial ideology. With regard to the moral message, Daniel and his friends are clearly presented as a model of how the Judean exiles can be faithful to their God while still engaging with the pagan culture of the court rather than withdrawing from it. Both this and the subversion of imperial ideology encourages the Judeans to maintain their ethnic and religious identity as those who live faithfully in a covenant relationship with the God of their ancestors, who is the Most High God.[10]

Questions

1. How did you understand the book of Daniel when you first heard these stories as a child? How did you understand it when read it as an adult? Has reading different interpretations of the book helped you to understand it better, and if so, how?

2. Why is it so important to understand the context or contexts in which the book was written? And how does understanding

---

10. Lucas, personal correspondence.

Part III: What Is the Message of Daniel for Today?

    these contexts help us to relate the message of the book to different contexts today?

3. How easy do you find it to accept a new and different way of interpreting something in the Bible? Does accepting a new interpretation challenge your beliefs about the inspiration and authority of the Bible?

8

Daniel has little or nothing to say about events in the Middle East in the twentieth and twenty-first centuries

Why is it that many Christians believe that the Bible contains predictions that have been fulfilled in recent history? There are several stages to their argument:

- It starts with God's promise of the land to Abraham and his descendants as "an everlasting inheritance" (Gen 12:3; 17:3–8). This is understood to mean that the Jewish people have a divine right to the land for all time.

- Prophecies in the Old Testament about the return of Jewish exiles to the land after the Babylonian exile in the sixth century BC were fulfilled in the return in 538 BC. But they have been fulfilled *once again* in the twentieth century. The return of Jews to the land through the Zionist movement and the creation of the State of Israel should be seen as clear fulfillments of promises and prophecies in the Old Testament.

- The visions of Daniel are looking forward not only to the first coming of Christ, but also to his second coming. They envisage a time when Jews have returned to the land, and when the temple in Jerusalem has been restored. Many also believe that the whole sacrificial system will be reinstated.

- Christians should therefore see the creation of the State of Israel in 1948 and the capture of East Jerusalem and the temple mount by Israeli forces in 1967 as significant events leading up to the second coming of Christ. Some (though certainly not all) go further and believe that the Dome of the Rock, which was built on the site of the Jewish temple, will have to be destroyed to enable the temple to be rebuilt on this site.

- Everything that has happened in Palestine since Jews began to settle Palestine in the 1880s until the present time fits into the way the Bible predicts that history will unfold.

As we have already seen in Part II, these are the assumptions that underlie Walvoord's interpretation of the book of Daniel:

> Today, when attention is again being riveted upon the Middle East, and particularly upon Israel, these issues are not merely of academic interest because they are the key to the present movement of history in anticipation of what lies ahead.[1]

> For Christians living in the age of grace and searching for understanding of these difficult days that may be bringing to a close God's purpose in His church, the book of Daniel casts a broad light on contemporary events foreshadowing the consummation. If God is reviving His people Israel politically, allowing the church to drift into indifference and apostasy, and permitting the nations to move towards centralization of political power, it may not be long before the time of the end will overtake the world.[2]

> The present occupation of Jerusalem by Israel may be a preparatory step to the reestablishment of the Mosaic system of sacrifices. Obviously sacrifices cannot be

---

1. Walvoord, *Daniel*, 217.
2. Walvoord, *Daniel*, 382–83.

Daniel has little or nothing to say about events in the Middle East

> stopped and a temple cannot be desecrated unless both are in operation.[3]

Is there a convincing alternative to this way of using the Bible—and Daniel in particular—to interpret the history of the Middle East? This other approach, which is adopted in this book, can be summarized in the following way:

- The Old Testament looks forward to the coming of the kingdom of God, and New Testament writers believe that the kingdom of God came—or began to come—through the life, death, and resurrection of Jesus. When the good news about Jesus was accepted by gentiles, they became part of the people of God and therefore shared all the blessings of the original covenant made with Abraham. This means that the promise made to Abraham about his descendants and about the promised land were fulfilled in the coming of the kingdom of God in Jesus. Gentile believers were therefore grafted into the nation of Israel, and the church needs to be seen as the continuation of Israel—Israel that has been restored and renewed in Jesus the Messiah. Since promises about the nation were so closely associated with promises about the land, the promise of the land had to be re-interpreted. It was therefore expanded to include all lands, and seen as a way of describing the inheritance enjoyed by every believer. For Christians, therefore, reading the Old Testament through the eyes of the New Testament means that promises and prophecies in the Old Testament about the nation of Israel and the promised land do not apply exclusively today to the Jewish people and the land of Israel.[4]

- In the visions in the second half of Daniel, the main focus is on the situation in Palestine in the 160s BC, when the country is in the power of an autocratic ruler who attempts to suppress the Jewish people and their religion. The main message for suffering Jewish communities in Palestine is that they will

3. Walvoord, *Daniel*, 288–89.
4. See Chapman, *Christian Zionism and the Restoration of Israel*, 53–88.

soon be delivered. This is how the main message of Daniel is summed up by Goldingay;

> The revelations in Daniel 10–12 and elsewhere are substantially shaped by the Scriptures themselves; it was these Scriptures which mediated the author's God-given understanding to him.... It is the Scriptures which are the seer's source of insight. They enable him to make sense of past, present, and future for his people. The past they have been through (the rule of foreign empires over Judea, the comings and goings of the Hellenistic period, the sufferings of the Antiochene period) seems impossible to understand, but the Scripture helps the seer to make sense of them. The Seleucid oppression is like that of the Assyrians: as the latter fell, so will the former. The temple desecration is like that during the Exile: as that was reversed, so will this one be. The affliction brought upon people by Antiochus is like that of Yahweh's servant in Isaiah: in this case, too, it will give way to triumph.[5]

- The book of Daniel and other books in the Old Testament and the New Testament therefore do not provide detailed predictions about how history is going to unfold. If we believe in the sovereignty of God in history, the return of Jews to the land and the creation of the State of Israel must have some meaning. But they cannot be interpreted as fulfillments of promises and prophecies in the Bible.

- When Christians today try to understand all that has happened in the Middle East, they need to understand this history in the same way that they understand any other history. They should evaluate the history of the Israeli-Palestinian conflict and how it has developed in recent years in the same way that they evaluate other history. If they make moral judgments about Israel and the Palestinians, they should apply the same kind of criteria that they use in other contexts. If they are concerned about issues of justice, they will want to apply

---

5. Goldingay, *Daniel*, Word Biblical Themes, 41–42.

Daniel has little or nothing to say about events in the Middle East widely accepted understandings of human rights and international law.

Using Daniel and other books of the Bible to chart how history is going to develop—especially in the Middle East—and how the world is going to end certainly provides many with simple, clear-cut answers to questions about all the suffering and injustice that we see in the world. But it probably isn't the kind of answer that the writers of the Bible wanted to give. There must be other ways of using our minds to understand contemporary history and to relate the message of the Bible to what is happening around us.[6]

Questions

1. What do you see and the strengths and weaknesses of the approach that uses the Bible to interpret the significance of what has been happening in the Middle East since the beginning of the twentieth century?

2. What do you see as the strengths and weaknesses of the approach that believes that promises and prophecies about the nation and the land in the Old Testament were fulfilled in the coming of the kingdom of God in Jesus? Does this mean that these promises and prophecies cannot therefore be used to interpret the return of Jews to the land in the Zionist movement and the creation of the State of Israel?

---

6. See Chapman, *Christian Zionism and the Restoration of Israel*, 94–102; Chapman, *Whose Promised Land?*

9

The hope that is based on the resurrection of Christ is greater and stronger than the hope that was offered to Daniel

If Daniel was written in the sixth century BC, what kind of hope would the book have held out to its readers? They would have been heartened to know that their exile in Babylon was soon about to end. But the enigmatic response to Daniel's prayer that came through the angel Gabriel warned that even after the return there would be testing times ahead. For those who would be martyred in the persecution that was to come, there was the confident hope of resurrection and vindication beyond the grave.

If the book came together in its final form in the second century BC, the clear message was that the time of persecution and suffering under Antiochus was going to end soon: "At that time your people shall be delivered" (12:2). The people would regain their freedom, the temple would be cleansed, and the sacrificial system would be reinstated. Since many had already been martyred because of their refusal to renounce their Jewish faith with all its traditions, there was an assurance that death was not the end but would be followed by some kind of resurrection.

What kind of hopes do the writers of the New Testament hold out to their readers? What difference does the coming of Christ

The hope that is based on the resurrection of Christ

make today to our hopes for the future? There are two books in the New Testament that were written to encourage Christians who were already experiencing—or about to experience—extreme suffering.

The first, 1 Peter, was written to Christians in Asia Minor who were beginning to suffer persecution for their faith. Peter can offer a much surer ground for hope than Daniel could, because of what Jesus had achieved through his death and resurrection. Peter tells them: "Beloved, do not be surprised at the fiery ordeal that is taking place among you to test you, as though something strange were happening to you" (1 Pet 4:12). The hope that he holds out to them is based on the resurrection of Jesus: "Blessed be the God and Father of our Lord Jesus Christ! By his great mercy he has given us a new birth into a living hope through the resurrection of Jesus Christ from the dead, into an inheritance that is imperishable, undefiled, and unfading, kept in heaven for you" (1 Pet 1:3–4). While Daniel had written that "many shall be purified, cleansed and refined" (11:35), Peter tells his readers that they can rejoice, "even if not for a little while you have had to suffer various trials, so that the genuineness of your faith—being more precious than gold that, though perishable is tested by fire—may be found to result in praise and glory and honor when Jesus Christ is revealed" (1 Pet 1:6–7). This conviction about the second coming of Christ takes us far beyond the hope that was offered to Daniel: "in accordance with his promise, we wait for new heavens and a new earth, where righteousness is at home" (2 Pet 3:13).

We have already seen (in I.9) the extent to which the book of Revelation is indebted to Daniel. Daniel holds out the hope that the tyranny under a cruel autocrat will come to an end, and that even if the people of God do not experience deliverance in this life, they can look forward to resurrection and vindication beyond the grave. John in Revelation hears the risen Christ saying to him: "Do not be afraid; I am the first and the last, and the living one. I was dead, and see, I am alive forever and ever; and I have the keys of Death and of Hades" (Rev 1:17–18).

While Daniel's visions look forward to the fall of Antiochus and his empire, John in Revelation offers a vivid picture of the fall of the Roman Empire. In chapter 13, in language that is very similar to Daniel's description of Antiochus (11:36–39), Rome is described as a beast that blasphemes against God and has power over the whole world:

> And I saw a beast coming out of the sea. He had ten horns and seven heads, with ten crowns on his horns, and on each head a blasphemous name.... The whole world was astonished and followed the beast. Men worshiped the dragon because he had given authority to the beast, and they also worshiped the beast and asked, "Who is like the beast? Who can make war against him?"
>
> The beast was given a mouth to utter proud words and blasphemies and to exercise his authority for forty-two months. He opened his mouth to blaspheme God, and to slander his name and his dwelling places and those who live in heaven. He was given power to make war against the saints and to conquer them. And he was given authority over every tribe, people, language, and nation. All the inhabitants of the earth will worship the beast—all whose names have not been written in the book of life belonging to the Lamb that was slain from the creation of the world. (Rev 13:1–8)

In Revelation 17, Rome is described as "the great prostitute, who sits on many waters. With her the kings of the earth committed adultery and the inhabitants of the earth were intoxicated with the wine of her adulteries" (17:1–2). And, in words that would have sounded unbelievable to those in John's time who were still suffering under Rome, what follows is a jubilant cry that follows the fall of Rome:

> Fallen! Fallen is Babylon the Great!... For all the nations have drunk the maddening wine of her adulteries. (Rev 17:2–3)
>
> Hallelujah! Salvation and glory and power belong to our God, for true and just are his judgments. He has condemned the great prostitute who corrupted the earth by

The hope that is based on the resurrection of Christ

her adulteries. He has avenged on her the blood of his servants. (Rev 19:1–2)

In chapter 21 John looks even further ahead when he sees "a new heaven and a new earth" (Rev 21:1). He has clearly understood very well the hope that Daniel was given, but, because of his understanding of the work of Christ in his death and resurrection, he is able to offer a much fuller and more certain hope than was given to Daniel.

Questions

1. What kind of hope did the book of Daniel hold out to its original readers? What basis did they have for trusting that God was still in control and that their future was secure?
2. If the book of Daniel holds out the hope of vindication of the faithful—either here or through resurrection "to everlasting life" (12:2)—how does the New Testament fill out this hope?
3. Why is it that 1 Peter and Revelation are able to offer a much fuller and more confident hope than Daniel was able to offer?

10

Daniel is a call to discernment, faithfulness, perseverance, and watchfulness

Having tried to work through some of the issues in interpreting this book, we need to face up to some of the very personal challenges that it presents. And it shouldn't be hard for us to see how each of these challenges is echoed and developed by the writers of the New Testament.

Discernment

Daniel is marked out from the beginning of the book as someone who possesses wisdom. Nebuchadnezzar's staff are asked to find among the Jewish exiles "young men . . . endowed with knowledge and insight" (1:4). After their induction programme at the palace, we are told that "To these four young men God gave knowledge and skill in every aspect of literature and wisdom; Daniel also had insight into all visions and dreams" (1:17). They must have begun to understand how the Babylonian government worked and what was going on in the surrounding nations.

We're also told that Daniel was always keen to understand the meaning of the visions that he received: "he understood the word, having received understanding of the vision" (10:1). The angel

Daniel is a call to discernment

who appears to him says, "Do not fear, Daniel, for from the first day that you set your mind to gain understanding and to humble yourself before God . . . I . . . have come to help you understand what is to happen to your people at the end of days" (10:14). At the very end of the book he is still seeking a better understanding of what God is saying to him about the future: "I heard but could not understand; so I said, 'My lord, what shall be the outcome of these things?'" (12:8). Daniel is therefore not only worldly wise because of his role at the heart of government; he is desperate to understand as best he can how God is at work in the world around him.

We have already seen (in I.1) that Daniel's visions describe a situation in which some of the Jewish community in Palestine are prepared to cooperate with Antiochus: "He shall seduce with intrigue those who violate the covenant" (11:32). Those who are not prepared to cooperate are described as "the wise": "But the people who are loyal to their God shall stand firm and take action. The wise among the people shall give understanding to many. . . . Some of the wise shall fall, so that they may be refined, purified, and cleansed, until the time of the end" (11:32-35). "None of the wicked shall understand, but those who are wise shall understand" (12:10). The book of Daniel is therefore calling its readers to understand the real issues at stake in their situation and to remain faithful to God. This is why Lacocque has suggested that "One of the most important contributions of the book of Daniel is its new insistence on the link between faith and intelligence."[1]

Could the example of Daniel, therefore, challenge Christians today to think more seriously about what is happening in our own societies and in the wider world—like climate change and the environment, the increasing gap between rich and poor, increasing conflict between nations, and migration and immigration? Should some of us be taking a keener interest in social and political issues in our own countries? While few of us are walking the corridors of power in the way that Daniel was, do we know who to turn to if we want to understand the changing relationships between world powers like the USA, Russia, and China? Paul encouraged the

---

1. Quoted in Baldwin, *Daniel*, 187.

Christians at Rome to develop what has been called "the Christian mind": "Do not be conformed to this world, but be transformed by the renewing of your minds, so that you may discern what is the will of God—what is good and acceptable and perfect" (Rom 12:2). Daniel should be for us a model of what it means to strive for discernment and wisdom.

Faithfulness

The book of 1 Maccabees describes how Antiochus attempted to eradicate completely the practices of Judaism, and to impose Greek cultural practices on the whole population. It begins by describing how many Jews cooperated with the whole programme of Hellenization:

> In those days certain renegades came out from Israel and misled many, saying, "Let us go and make a covenant with the Gentiles around us, for since we separated from them many disasters have come upon us." This proposal pleased them, and some of the people eagerly went to the king, who authorised them to observe the ordinances of the Gentiles. So they built a gymnasium in Jerusalem, according to Gentile custom, and removed the marks of circumcision, and abandoned the holy covenant. They joined with the Gentiles and sold themselves to do evil. (1 Macc 1:11–15)

Antiochus was imposing his pagan religion as a way of uniting his empire, and accepting his programme meant that Jews were stopping temple worship, ceasing to observe the Sabbath, and abandoning the practice of circumcision:

> Then the king wrote to his whole kingdom that all should be one people, and that all should give up their particular customs. All the Gentiles accepted the command of the king. Many even from Israel gladly adopted his religion; they sacrificed to idols and profaned the Sabbath. And the king sent letters by messengers to Jerusalem and the towns of Judah; he directed them to follow customs

Daniel is a call to discernment

strange to the land, to forbid burnt offerings and sacrifices and drink offerings in the sanctuary, to profane Sabbaths and festivals, to defile the sanctuary and the priests, to build altars and sacred precincts and shrines for idols, to sacrifice swine and other animals, and to leave their sons uncircumcised. They were to make themselves abominable by everything unclean and profane, so that they would forget the law and change all the ordinances. He added, "And whoever does not obey the command of the king shall die." (1 Macc 1:41–50)

In New Testament times Christians were faced with the same kind of demand that Antiochus had made. They were required to profess their allegiance to the Roman emperor by declaring "Caesar is Lord." If they were prepared to resist this demand and declare that "Jesus is Lord," they would sometimes have to pay for it with their own lives. There are many situations today where Christians are faced with demands to express total allegiance to the state, and where this becomes a test of their faithfulness. In all their different situations, where can they go along with what is asked of them, and where do they need to draw the line and stand firm?

Perseverance and watchfulness

This book is able to call for perseverance because one of its basic messages is that, in the words of Goldingay, "Daniel looks in the face of the possibility of human power and arrogance toppling the rule of heaven over the world. It affirms that the powers of heaven may be assailed and hurt, but that God will still reserve the last word."[2] The book ends therefore with a blessing that is pronounced on those who remain faithful: "Happy are those who persevere and attain the thousand three hundred thirty-five days" (12:12). Daniel is assured of the future that awaits him in this way: "But you, go your way, and rest; you shall rise for your reward at the end of the days" (12:13).

---

2. Goldingay, *Daniel*, Word Biblical Themes, 103.

Part III: What Is the Message of Daniel for Today?

This call to perseverance is echoed in the accounts of Jesus' eschatological discourse in the three Synoptic Gospels: "He who endures to the end will be saved" (Mark 13:13; cf. Matt 24:13; Luke 21:19). When Jesus is speaking about the future in the days before his death, his main focus is on the coming destruction of Jerusalem, which was to take place in 70 AD, and on the persecution that the disciples would experience. In Mark's account this main part of the discourse ends with the words "Truly I tell you, this generation will not pass away until all these things have taken place. Heaven and earth will pass away, but my words will not pass away" (Mark 13:30–31). He goes on to speak about the more distant future and his second coming when he says "But about *that day or hour* no one knows, neither the angels in heaven, nor the Son, but only the Father" (Mark 13:32, emphasis added). Because he gives no clues about the timing of "that day," he simply goes on to ask for watchfulness: "Beware, keep alert; for you do not know when the time will come. . . . Therefore, keep awake. . . . And what I say to you, I say to all: Keep awake" (Mark 13:33–37; cf. Matt 24:36–44; Luke 21:34–36).

The book of Revelation has more similarities with Daniel than any other Old Testament book. The letters to the seven churches in Asia Minor are pastoral letters addressed to Christians to prepare them for the intense suffering they are about to face. Several of these letters end with encouragements to persevere and be watchful: "To everyone who conquers and continues to do my works to the end, I will give authority over the nations; to rule them with an iron rod . . . even as I also received authority from my Father" (Rev 2:26–28). "To the one who conquers I will give a place with me on my throne, just as I myself conquered and sat down with my Father on his throne" (3:21).

Questions

1. If Daniel was marked out for his wisdom and discernment, what are the big issues over which Christians need to be searching for wisdom and discernment today? What are

some of the issues in your own country and in the world that call for special discernment?

2. What does it mean in your context today to remain faithful? What are the particular areas where you may have to draw the line and take a stand—whatever the cost?

3. What are the things in your situation that make perseverance and watchfulness difficult? How do New Testament writers reinforce Daniel's message about perseverance?

Postscript

Daniel is told no less than three times that he is "greatly beloved" (9:23; 10:11, 19). Perhaps what is ultimately most important for Daniel, therefore, is not his gifts or what he knows or what he does, but his relationship with God. He knows that he is loved by God.

Is it too much to hope that, if we are attempting to walk in the footsteps of Daniel, we can hear these same words *addressed to each one of us*: "Do not fear, greatly beloved, you are safe. Be strong and courageous!" (12:19)?

Bibliography

Anderson, Robert A. *Daniel: Signs and Wonders*. Grand Rapids: Eerdmans, 1984.
Baldwin, Joyce G. *Daniel: An Introduction and Commentary*. TOTC. Downers Grove, IL: InterVarsity, 1978.
Bauckham, Richard. *The Climax of Prophecy: Studies in the Book of Revelation*. London: T. & T. Clark, 1998
Bruce, F. F. *1 & 2 Thessalonians*. WBC 45. Dallas: Word, 1982.
Calvin, John. *A Commentary on Daniel*. Vol. 2. Edinburgh: Banner of Truth, 1986.
Caird, G. B. *The Revelation of St. John the Divine*. London: Black, 1971.
Chapman, Colin. *Christian Zionism and the Restoration of Israel: How Should We Interpret the Scriptures?* Eugene, OR: Cascade, 2021.
———. *Whose Promised Land? The Continuing Conflict Over Israel and Palestine*. 5th ed. London: SPCK, 1924.
Collins, John J. *Daniel: A Commentary on the Book of Daniel*. Hermeneia. Minneapolis: Fortress, 1993.
Di Lella, Alexander A. *The Book of Daniel: A New Translation with Notes and Commentary on Chapters 10–12*. AB 23. New York: Doubleday, 1978.
Goldingay, John. *Daniel*. Rev. ed. WBC 30. Grand Rapids: Zondervan, 2019.
———. *Daniel*. Word Biblical Themes. Dallas: Word, 1989.
———. *Daniel and the Twelve Prophets for Everyone*. London: SPCK, 2016.
Hummel, Daniel G. *The Rise and Fall of Dispensationalism*. Grand Rapids: Eerdmans, 2023.
Lucas, Ernest C. *Daniel*. ApOTC. Leicester, UK: Apollos, 2002.
McDermott, Gerald R. *The New Christian Zionism: Fresh Perspectives on Israel and the Land*. Downers Grove, IL: IVP Academic, 2016.
Morris, Leon. *1 Corinthians*. Tyndale NT Commentary. Downers Grove, IL: InterVarsity, 1985.
Newson, Carol A. *Daniel: A Commentary*. OTL. Louisville: John Knox, 2014.
Wallace, Ronald S. *The Lord Is King: The Message of Daniel*. Downers Grove, IL: InterVarsity, 1979.
Walvoord, John F. *Daniel*. The John Walvoord Prophecy Commentaries. Chicago: Moody, 2012.
Wright, Christopher J. H. *Hearing the Message of Daniel: Sustaining Faith in Today's World*. Grand Rapids: Zondervan, 2017.

Subject Index

Abednego, 105, 128
abomination of desolation, vi, 7, 25, 31, 38, 48–49, 88, 90–91, 99
Abraham, 77, 82, 97, 141, 143
Adam, 53–54
Akkadian, 66
Al-Aqsa, 88
Alexander, 13–14, 24, 84, 86–87
Allegory, 123
Anabaptist, 125
Antichrist, vi, 53, 74, 84, 92–94
Antiochus, v-vi, xi, 3–9, 11, 13, 20–22, 25–26, 30–33, 37, 39, 44, 47–48, 51, 53–54, 56, 58–59, 61, 63, 65, 69–70, 75, 84–85, 89–93, 99, 101, 108–9, 111, 116–18, 120, 124–25, 131, 133–36, 138, 144, 146–48, 151–53
apocalyptic, 29, 54, 58, 74, 81
Apocrypha, 3
Appian, 7
Aramaic, 1, 34, 48, 65
Asia Minor, 59, 147, 154
Assyria, 20, 22, 144
authoritarian, vii, 127–32
authority, 53, 57, 61, 133, 137, 140, 154
authorship, v, xii-xiii, 1, 63, 66, 118
autocratic, xii, 132, 143, 147
Azariah, 104, 116

Babylon, xi, 1, 8–10, 15, 17–18, 23, 28–30, 34, 38, 41, 51, 63, 68, 70, 73, 83, 91, 98, 101, 103–6, 108, 111–12, 116–20, 128, 131, 135–36, 141, 146, 148, 150
beast(s), vi, 12–13, 16–17, 38, 56, 60, 82, 86–87, 98–99, 121, 148
Belshazzar, xii, 10, 32, 38–39, 41, 109, 127–32
Bible, ix-x, 64, 68, 72, 97, 133, 141–42, 145
blasphemy, 4, 21, 32, 93, 148

Canaanite, 17
Chaldeans, 104, 130
chiasm, chiastic, 35–36
Christ, Jesus, xii, 28, 32–33, 40, 42–43, 45–47, 51–53, 55–66, 68, 71, 74, 76–79, 81–83, 87, 89–90, 93–95, 97, 99, 125, 143, 145–49, 153,
Christian Zionism, ix, 72
chronology, 26–27, 31, 71
chronography, 26, 31–32
church, vi, 46, 52, 54, 59–61, 71, 74, 76–77, 83–85, 95–97, 99, 120, 142
conflict, ix, 11, 38, 52, 58–61, 96, 98, 101, 115, 144

Subject Index

covenant, 18, 31, 60–61, 74, 77, 111, 114, 151–52
creation, 16–17, 46, 53
Cyprus, 20
Cyrus, 20, 30, 38, 103, 117

Darius, xii, 117
deliverance, vii, xii, 13, 31, 34–36, 51, 55, 70, 113, 119–20, 122–26, 128, 146–47
Devil, 59–60, 94
dispensational, dispensationlism, vi, xii–xiii, 58, 70–99, 101
Dome of the Rock, 88, 142
dream, 10, 12, 35, 37–39, 41–42, 44, 57, 78, 105, 107, 109, 128, 113–14

Egypt, xi, 7, 13, 15, 20, 63, 68, 114
Elijah, 60
End, the, 1, 10–11, 33, 49, 51, 68, 74, 88, 91, 95–96
end times, vi, ix, 88, 52,
eschatology, eschatological, 32, 45, 49, 60, 84, 154
Esther, 60
Europe, 120
exile, vi, 15, 18–19, 21, 24, 28–31, 34, 57, 65, 68, 75, 88–89, 99, 103–4, 106, 111, 113, 116–17, 128, 141, 144, 146, 150
Ezra, 19, 30

fiery furnace, xi, 41, 105, 122–23
first coming of Christ, v–vi, 27–32, 56, 78, 83–85, 141, 146–47
fulfill, fulfillment, vi, 17, 24, 32–33, 49, 51, 56, 68–70, 73–74, 78–79, 81, 84, 87–89, 92–93, 95, 97, 114, 141, 143–45

Gabriel, 10, 19, 21–22, 25, 29, 31, 57, 76, 88, 113, 146
gentile, 4–6, 20, 74, 76–78, 84, 97, 132, 143, 152

Greece, Greek, v–vi, 11–14, 37–38, 65, 86–87, 98–99, 152

Hananiah, 104, 116
Hanukkah, 8
Hebrew, 1, 15–16, 34, 50, 65
Hellenization, 118, 152
history, vii, ix, xii, 20–22, 25, 28, 32–34, 39–40, 42, 57, 60, 66–67, 69, 71, 73, 81, 83, 87, 97–99, 101, 107–8, 119, 123, 127, 132, 141–44
horn(s), 6, 13, 38, 43–44, 56, 59, 86, 93, 109, 124, 142, 144–45, 148

incarnation, 58
inspiration, 133, 137, 140
interpretation, v–vii, xi–xiii, 1, 10, 13, 15, 31–32, 34–39, 44, 48, 65–66, 70–99, 101, 112, 114, 116, 118, 130, 133–40, 150
Isaac, 77, 82

Israel (Bible), vi, ix, 4, 17, 21, 24, 27–28, 42, 45–46, 58, 71, 74, 76–77, 87–88, 92–93, 95–97, 99, 104, 112, 114, 117, 124, 129–31, 141–45, 152
Israel (State of), vi, ix–x, 24, 72, 88, 95–99, 142, 144–45
Islam, 24

Jacob, 77, 82
Japan, Japanese, 36, 119
Jehoiakim, 108, 127
Jerusalem, v–vi, xiii, 4, 7, 17, 19, 21–22, 27–33, 38, 42, 45, 48, 53, 58, 65, 68–70, 74, 76–77, 79, 88, 90–91, 96–97, 99, 103, 112–13, 116–18, 127, 129, 141–42, 152, 154
Jesus Christ, see Christ, Jesus
Jews, Jewish, vi, xi, 4, 7, 11, 13, 20, 22, 29–30, 32, 34–37, 39,

Subject Index

65, 68–69, 74, 77, 84, 95–98, 101, 103, 111, 116–18, 120, 124, 128–29, 131–32, 141, 143–46, 151–52
Joseph, 15
Josephus, 7, 12–13,
Joshua, 30
Jubilee, 19, 25, 31–32,
Judah, 4, 22, 108, 127, 152
Judaism, 4, 6, 152
Jupiter, 7

Kairos Document, 120
kingdom of God, vi, 13, 16, 41–43, 54, 57, 60, 77–79, 82, 86, 97–99, 101, 111, 143, 145
Kittim, 20
Korea, 119–20

land, vi, 4, 17–19, 21, 24–25, 29–30, 33, 35, 37–39, 45–46, 57, 76, 95–98, 113–14, 141, 143–45, 153
law, 4, 5–6, 16, 19, 93, 105, 114, 118
Lebanon, ix
Libya, 20
lions' den, xi, 112–13, 117, 122, 124
literal, v-vi, 8, 23–24, 56, 62, 71, 73–75, 78, 80–81, 88–89, 99, 123
Livy, 7, 123

Maccabeus, Judas, 5, 7
Maccabees, Maccabean, 8, 84, 125, 135
Macedonia, 13, 87
martyr, martyrdom, 54, 60–61, 81, 118, 124, 131, 146
Media, 11, 13, 38, 98
Meshach, 105, 128
Messiah, 28, 45, 57, 68, 79, 143
Mesopotamia, 17, 66
Michael, 58–59
Middle East, vi-vii, ix-x, 87, 95–97, 99, 141–45

millennium, vi, xii, 61, 71, 80–83, 99, 101
miracle, miraculous, vii, xii, 34, 55, 119, 123–25, 131
Mishael, 104, 116
Moses, 58, 60, 88, 105

nationalism, 106
nations, ix, 18, 28, 44–45, 47, 57, 59, 61, 63, 65, 71, 78, 80, 96, 98, 107–9, 112, 131, 142, 151, 154
Nazism, 106
Near East, 26, 36, 66, 138
Nebuchadnezzar, xii, 10, 12, 15, 35–36, 38–39, 41–42, 57, 78, 103–6, 108–9, 112, 114, 116–17, 122–23, 127–32, 150
Nehemiah, 19, 30
New Testament, 1, 4, 28, 40, 54–58, 76–77, 89, 93, 97, 143–44, 146–47, 149, 150–55
numbers, v-vi, 1, 23–26, 31, 73–75, 81, 99, 107

Old Testament, 4, 8, 15, 22, 27, 40–41, 46–47, 50–56, 62, 65–68, 72, 75–77, 85, 95, 97–98, 120, 141, 143–45, 154
Onias, 7, 31

Palestine, Palestinian, ix, xi, 1, 3, 6, 8–9, 13, 33, 51, 63, 68, 87, 96, 98, 101, 111, 116–18, 120, 131, 135–36, 142–44, 151
persecution, vii, x, 1, 20, 23, 28, 46, 54, 61, 101, 116, 122–26, 135, 146
Persia, Persian, 11, 18, 29, 37–38, 59, 65, 84, 98, 103, 117
Pharaoh, 15
political, vii, 81, 96–98, 116–21, 136, 142, 151
Polybius, 7, 20
Porphyry, 7, 137

161

Subject Index

prayer, vii, 14, 17–18, 25, 28–29, 31–32, 76, 88, 110, 112–15, 146
prediction, vi, xi, 8, 22, 51, 53, 56, 63–67, 69–70, 73, 93, 95, 124, 137–38, 141
prophecy, vi, 8, 23–24, 29, 30, 32–33, 51, 64–66, 68–69, 72, 74, 76, 83–84, 92–93, 95–97, 137, 141, 144–45
promises, 8, 30, 76, 95, 97, 144–45
pseudonymous, 66
Ptolemies, 13, 38, 84

quasi-predictive prophecy, 8, 20, 65–66

redemption, 17
repentance, 18, 25, 28, 60, 109, 114, 129
restoration, v, ix, 19, 21, 27–32, 70, 76, 88, 113–15
resurrection, vii, 42, 45, 50–51, 53, 55, 68, 79, 125, 143, 146–47, 149
Rome, Romans, v–vi, 7, 12–14, 24, 42, 48, 54, 56, 60–61, 86–87, 90, 94, 99, 119, 121, 136, 148, 152–53

Sabbath, 4, 17–18, 24–25, 118, 152–53
sacrifice, 4–5, 30, 38, 49, 57–58, 74, 88–89, 95–96, 142, 146, 153
Satan, 59–60, 81, 94
Saul, 46, 52
Scripture, ix, 4, 8, 20–22, 67–68, 70–72, 81, 97, 112–13, 133, 137–38, 144
second coming of Christ, v–vi, 27–32, 45, 58, 71, 74, 78–87, 89–90, 95, 97, 101, 141–42, 147
Seleucids, 3, 7, 13–14, 38, 56, 84, 86–87, 144

Shadrach, 105, 128
Solomon, 58, 112–13
Son of Man, vi, 16, 35, 38, 40, 43–47, 50, 52, 56–57, 60, 78–80, 97–98
sovereignty of God, vii, xii, 39–41, 80, 97, 107–11, 114, 119, 122–26, 129, 131–32, 134–35, 144–45
suffering, vii, xii, 11, 25–26, 44, 46–47, 59–61, 116, 119, 147, 154
symbol, symbolic, 24–26, 33, 42, 56, 58, 62, 75–76, 81–82, 107, 113
Syria, xi, 13–14, 63, 68, 87

tabernacle, 58
temple, v–vi, 4–9, 11, 19, 25–27, 29–32, 38, 48, 52–53, 57–58, 61, 74, 79, 84–85, 88–91, 92, 96, 99, 112–13, 118, 129, 142, 144, 146, 152
thrones, 46, 51, 61
Titus, vi, 48, 90
torah, 17
type, typology, 51, 92–93

vision(s), xi, 3, 10–12, 30, 34–36, 38–39, 43, 46, 49, 58–60, 63, 69, 77–79, 92, 99, 101, 107, 118–19, 123–24, 126, 133, 141, 150

weeks, seventy, 19, 25, 30–31, 38, 51, 74, 76, 88, 134

Yahweh, 32, 41, 114, 144

Zerubbabel, 30
Zeus, 4, 7, 48, 91, 118
Zionism, ix, 95–96, 98, 141, 145
Zion, 6, 22

Author Index

Anderson, Robert A., 30, 40

Baldwin, Joyce G., 3, 15–16, 21, 24, 28, 32, 34–35, 40, 44, 46, 50, 57, 59, 64, 69, 98, 107, 109, 117, 123–24, 129–30, 151
Bauckham, Richard, 60
Blake, William, 128
Breed, Brennan W., 135
Bruce, F. F., 53

Calvin, John, xii, 27
Caird, G. B., 55–56, 62
Chapman, Colin, 45, 47, 77, 81, 97, 143, 145
Collins, John J., 96
Cranfield, C. E. B., 32

Darby, John Nelson, xii
De Lella, Alexander A.,108, 111

Goldingay, John, 4, 8, 10, 15, 20–24, 29–30, 33, 36, 41, 43–44, 47–49, 51–53, 55, 59, 65–70, 93, 109, 113, 115, 117–18, 123, 125, 131, 134, 144, 153

Hummell. Daniel G., 72

Irenaeus, 68

Lacoque, A., 34
Langlet, A., 34
Lucas, Ernest C., 3–4, 13, 17, 20–23, 25–27, 29, 32, 35, 37, 42, 45, 49, 66, 87, 104, 109–10, 119, 125, 129, 130–31, 134, 139

Mayer, J., 65
McDermott, Gerald R., 72
Montgomery, J. A., 27, 134
Morris, Leon, 54

Newsom, Carol, 29, 120, 132, 135
Newton, Isaac, 69

Pascal, Jean, 51, 68
Porphry, 137

Wallace, Ronald S., 4, 16, 28, 64, 104–5, 115, 130, 133, 136
Walvoord, John F., 66, 72–74, 76–78, 80–81, 83–84, 86–87, 89–90, 92–93, 95–96, 137, 142–43
Wright, Christopher, J. H., 134

Scripture Index

Genesis
1:26–27	16
12:3	141
17:3–8	141

Exodus
25:8	58
29:45–46	58

Leviticus
9:24	19
18	75
25–26	19, 75
25:2, 4	18
25:8–17	19, 25
25:38–55	32
26:21–28	18
26:33–35	18
26:40–43	18

Numbers
24:24	20
35:34	58

Deuteronomy
30:1–5	19

1 Kings
6:13	58
8:12	58
8:29–30	113

1 Chronicles
	17

2 Chronicles
	17
36:20–21	18, 24

Ezra
9:6–15	19

Nehemiah
1:5–11	19
9:5–37	19

Psalms
2	20
8:4	43
10:16	41
16:9–11	50
17:15	50
29:10	41
46	20

Scripture Index

Psalms (cont.)

47:2, 7	41
48	20
49:15	50
73:23–26	50
76	20
79	19
87:1–7	77
90:10	24
93:1	41
95:3	41
97:1	41
99:1	41
118:22	43

Isaiah

2:2–3	50
8:14–15	43
9:2–7	8
10	20
10:5–27	22
14:24–25	20
19	20, 77
23:15	24
26:19	50
31	20
40:1–2	21
52:13–15	22, 47, 50
53:11–12	23, 47, 50
56:6–8	77
65:1, 24	114

Jeremiah

25:11–12	17
29–32	20
29:4–7	103
29:10	17
37:17	xiii
43:8–13	20
46	20

Ezekiel

29–32	20
30:5	20
34–38	ix
38–39	20
47:21–23	77

Daniel

1–8	34, 104–6, 119–20, 127, 135, 150
1:17–21	104, 117, 150
2	12, 16, 35, 37–39, 86, 120, 135
2:17–19	112
2:19–23	55, 109, 114
2:28–29	10, 55
2:31–45	12, 42, 55, 57
2:39–45	10, 12, 24, 41–42, 57, 86, 110
2:47–48	104, 127
3	35, 122, 125
3:1–30	117
3:5	127
3:16–18	122
3:28	128
4	35
4:3	41, 128
4:17	xii, 41
4:22	107
4:25	128
4:30	128
4:33–37	41, 108, 128–29
5	35
5:1–5	129–30
5:11	130
5:20–23	109, 130
5:26–30	130
6	35, 122, 125
6:10	112

Scripture Index

6:28	117	9:24–27	7, 22, 24–25, 27–33, 48, 57, 73–77, 84–85, 88–91, 95, 108, 113, 134
6:30	131		
7	3, 6, 34–35, 37–39, 43, 46, 53, 69, 78, 86, 93, 97, 117–18, 135		
		10	38–39, 52, 65, 77, 124, 144
7:1–8	8, 12–13, 34, 44, 87, 109	10:1	103, 150, 156
		10:2	20–39, 84–85
7:9–10	46	10:3	105
7:11–12	8, 13, 44	10:5–6	56
7:13–14	vi, 24–25, 44–45, 47, 56–57, 60, 78–80, 98, 110	10:11–21	7–8, 39, 55, 59, 109, 151, 156–57
		10:27	7
7:15–28	8, 12–13, 27, 44, 78, 80, 110	11	3, 37–39, 86, 117–18, 135
7:19–28	6, 12, 23, 25, 27, 44, 46, 55–56, 59, 80, 87, 93, 98, 109–10, 124	11:2–39	7, 20, 84–85
		11:11	90
		11:17	86
		11:21–39	7–8, 11, 20, 48, 85, 91, 109
7:23–28	12, 23, 25, 27, 44, 55, 59, 80, 93, 98, 109, 124	11:32–37	7, 59, 84, 124, 151
		11:35–45	7–8, 11, 20, 49, 74, 84–85, 124, 147–48, 151
8	3, 30, 37, 86, 114, 118, 37–39, 41, 86, 118		
		12	3, 39, 52, 117, 144
8:8–14	3, 6–9, 13–14, 23–25, 48, 55	12:1–6	11, 13, 22, 24, 48–50, 55, 59, 110, 124–25, 146, 149
8:17–19	11, 49		
8:20–27	7, 11, 30–31, 55, 92, 108–9	12:7–9	11, 23, 25, 59, 124, 151
9	17, 28–29, 38–39, 76, 118	12:11–13	11, 23–24, 26, 48, 54–55, 60–61, 90–91, 153
9:1–4	17, 113–14		
9:4–23	28–29, 39, 85, 113–14, 156		
9:24	v, 19, 21, 23, 25, 27–33, 51, 57, 73–75, 88, 113, 134	12:19	156

Hosea

13:7–8	17

Scripture Index

Joel
2:20	20

Nahum
3:9	20

Zechariah
2:11	77
4:14	30
6:15	77
8:22–23	77
9:9–10	77
12:10—13:1	56
13:7	47
14	20
14:16–19	77

1 Maccabees
	3–7, 20, 124
1:10–15	7, 152
1:16–19	7
1:20–23	7
1:41–61	4–7, 153
2–4	7
4:36–59	8
4:41–61	5–6, 152–53

2 Maccabees
	3–4, 7
1:11–15	152
1:41–50	153
4:30–34	7
20	124

2 Esdras
12:11–12	13

Matthew
8:11–12	77, 82
19:28	46
24	49
24:13	154
24:15	48, 90
24:21	49
24:36–44	154
25:46	50
26:31	47

Mark
1:15	42, 79
2:10	43
2:28	43
8:31	47
9:12	47
10:45	47
13	40, 49
13:13–14	79, 154
13:19	49
13:21	49
13:26	45, 79
13:30–37	154
14:42	42
14:62	45
15:30	79

Luke
11:20	42, 79
19:10	43
20:17–18	43
21	49
21:19	154
21:22–23	49
21:26	x
21:34–36	154
22:28	46
23:27	68

John
1:14	89
2:13–22	89
5:25–29	50
10:16	77
17:20–22	46, 61

Scripture Index

Acts
1:3	42
9:4–5	46 52
28:31	42

Romans
5	54
11:17–24	77
12:2	152
13:1–7	121, 148

1 Corinthians
15	53–54
15:28	28

Galatians
3:26–29	77
6:16	97

Ephesians
1:10	28
2:11–23	52, 77
6:11–12	52, 115

Colossians
2:15	53

2 Thessalonians
2:1–12	53, 93

Hebrews
9:23—10:18	89

1 Peter
1:3–4	147
1:6–7	147
4:12–19	54, 147

2 Peter
3:13	147

1 John
	93
2:18, 22	93–94
4:3–4	94

Revelation
1:1–7	55–56, 59
1:17–18	55, 147
2:10	61
2:26–28	61, 154
3:10	61
3:21	61, 154
4:17–32	56
11:2–3	55, 61
11:15–17	19, 55, 57, 79
12:7–10	57, 59, 79
12:12	60
12:14	55
13:1–8	56, 124. 121, 128, 148
13:10	56
16:1	55
17:1–3	148
17:12	56
19:1–2	148–49
19:19	94
20:1–27	51, 55, 58, 61, 81, 89, 94, 149
22:10	55

www.ingramcontent.com/pod-product-compliance
Lightning Source LLC
Chambersburg PA
CBHW032156160426
43197CB00008B/937